Gastric Band Hypnosis For Women (2 in 1): Self-Hypnosis, Affirmations& Guided Meditations- Rapid Fat Burning, Healthy Eating Habits, Mindfulness, Confidence& Extreme Food Addiction

Rapid Weight Loss Hypnosis For Women: Self-Hypnosis& Guided Meditations- Extreme Fat Burning, Overcome Food Addiction& Emotional Eating+ Confidence& Self-Esteem Affirmations

Table of Contents

1. Guided Meditation Scripts

a. Guided Meditation Script for Weight Loss

Timings: 40-50 minutes

Welcome to your Guided Meditation training session for weight loss. This training is specially designed to enable you to achieve a healthy body, develop healthy eating habits, eating clean and exercise regularly. For best results, please give it your full attention and do not listen to it while doing activities where you need to maintain focus.

Now please make sure that you're seated in a comfortable chair, or lying down comfortably at a place where you will be undisturbed for some time. This guided meditation session will take about 40-50 minutes.

(NOTE: USE EYE FACSINATION INDUCTION)

{Sit comfortably in your chair or lay down comfortably in your bed. Make sure your head, neck, shoulders and knees are supported against the back of the chair or a pillow. Now I want you to find some point in your room and stare at it in a position where you are comfortable looking at it. Now keep on staring at that point. Keep staring…Keep Staring. Slowly you will start to notice that the more you stare at the point, the more your eyelids will start to get heavy and you will feel the urge to blink. The more you stare, the more your eyelids will get heavy and the urge to blink will get intense. Now blink your eyes slowly… Now blink again slowly… With each blink, your eyes will become heavy… heavy… so heavy and heavier… that due to this feeling of heaviness it will become difficult for you to keep your eyes open. Now because of this feeling of heaviness in your eyes, you will prefer your eyes to stay closed. Now close your eyes slowly and gently… Very slowly and gently. }

(OR USE HAND AND FINGER SPREADING INDUCTION)

{Now I want you to life up your arm and hand. Place the palm of your hand in front of your face. Make sure you are not wearing any glasses. Your palm should be at least 15 inches away from your face. Your hand fingers should be straight up and a bit above the eye level. Hold your elbow firmly. Now stare at your middle finger and let go of your hold on your elbow. Now keep on staring at your middle finger. Keep Staring. The more you stare at your middle finger the more you will feel that your fingers are starting to spread wider and wider. Now continue staring at your middle finger and you will feel that your hand is slowly pulling in towards your face as your fingers continue to spread. Slowly you will start to notice that the more you stare at the middle finger, your breathing will start to get deeper. And you will notice that the more your eyelids will start to get heavy and you will feel the urge to blink. The more you stare, the more your eyelids will get heavy and the urge to blink will get intense. Now blink your eyes slowly... Now blink again slowly... With each blink, your eyes will become heavy... heavy... so heavy and heavier... that due to this feeling of heaviness it will become difficult for you to keep your eyes open. Now because of this feeling of heaviness in your eyes, you will prefer your eyes to stay closed. Now close your eyes slowly and gently... Very slowly and gently. Now when your palm touches gently front of your face, you will bring your hand down and put in on your lap or belly or put it where ever you feel the comfortable position is for your hand. }

Now that your eyes are closed, put your one hand on your belly and another hand on your chest. As you inhale/breathe in you will feel your belly rising. And when you will exhale you will feel your belly lowering. Take a deep breath. Inhale slowly through your nose and then exhale slowly through your mouth. Feel the air going inside through your nose and feel the air coming outside through your mouth. If it is difficult for you to inhale through your nostrils then inhale through your mouth. Make sure to take a big deep breaths, not short and shallow breaths.

Take three deep breaths more. Inhale and then exhale. Inhale and then exhale. Inhale and then exhale. With every breath, you exhale you become very deeply relaxed. Now tense the muscles in your feet and then relax them slowly. Now tense the muscles in your calves and then relax them slowly. Now tense the muscles in your thighs and then relax them slowly. Now tense the muscles in your hips and then relax them slowly. Feel the relaxation and calmness moving upward from your feet to your calves towards your thighs and moving slowly towards your hips. You will feel nerves in your feet, calves, thighs, and hips deeply relaxing. Now tense the muscles in your belly and then relax them slowly. Now feel the soothing sensation of relaxation slowly moving your belly muscles. Now feel the deep sense of relaxation moving towards your chest. Your breathing will become very deep, gentle, and rhythmic. Now tense the muscles in your shoulders and then relax them slowly. Now this feeling of relaxation will move towards your shoulders and any tension in your shoulder will go away. Now feel this relaxation moving towards your neck slowly relaxing muscles there. Now tense the muscles in your arms and fingers and then relax them slowly. The feeling of relaxation will become deeper and deeper, and your arms, hand, fingers, and tips of fingernails will start to relax. This soothing feeling of relaxation will move towards your forehead. You will feel your eyelids getting relaxed. Now tense you jaw muscles and then relax them slowly. Your jaw muscles will relax and any tightness will be loosened. The feeling of calmness will flow to your cheeks and your entire body will become saturated with the sense of relaxation and calmness. Now gently place your hand over your heart and feel the gentle pressure warmth of your hand on your rising and falling chest. Feel the pulse of your heart. You will notice that any physical sensations of stress that you are holding in your body will be gone.

Now take a deep breath in and deep breath out, this will allow you to clear your mind from the today's events and thoughts. Just like snow wiping from a windscreen and resulting in a clearer sharp view. Any thoughts related to yesterday, today and tomorrow are now in the background of your attention. Your focus is here in the present moment that is filled with deep relaxation. With each deep breath, you take, you feel becoming deeply relaxed and in control of your mind and body by putting unwanted thoughts far away from the present moment. Just feel your breath for a while. When you notice your mind is wandering, bring back your attention to your breathing and feel your breath coming inside and going outside your body again.

And now I will count from ten down to zero. Each count will represent state of deep relaxation, and with each count down you will feel the deep calmness and relaxation in your body getting deeper and deeper. 10... 9...8...7...6...5...4...3...2...and 1... **(Snaps fingers)** Now deep sleep... Take few moments to let those feelings of calmness and relaxation soak you up. Let these feelings rejuvenate your mind and body. Your mind and body are ready to respond positively.

Now imagine yourself walking through a pathway lined with sparkling green magnificent trees and grass. It's a beautiful day to take a walk with the sunshine streaming through the trees, and the blue sky with beautiful white clouds above you. You can feel the soothing softness of grass beneath your feet. Now feel the cool comfortable breeze gently floating around you as you walk and you will notice your body and mind relaxing with each step you take. Hearing the birds chirping beautiful melody from the treetops, you stop a moment to listen to nature's wonders. Reaching out to lean against a tree, you can feel the rough texture of the bark of the tree and the smell of roses in the air. Take few moments to let those feelings of purification, calmness, and relaxation soak you up. Let these feelings rejuvenate your mind, body, and spirit. Your mind, body, and spirit are ready to respond positively. Now begin walking again and you will notice a small house located at the top of a long beautiful spiral staircase, with sides covered from green branches. The color of green branches will fill you with a soothing feeling of coolness and peace. Now continue walking towards that beautiful staircase. A feeling of calmness, relaxation will take over you. Now visualize the staircase as your pathway towards reaching your goal weight. Each step that you will take on this staircase will bring you closer to your desired weight goal.

Now stand at the 1st staircase and you will notice that you are becoming very motivated and determined to lose weight. You are becoming open to new positive thoughts and actions. You are very determined to bring a positive and healthy change to your lifestyle. You are going after what you want. You are in control of your life choices **(repeat twice).** Nothing can stop you from what you set your mind to **(repeat twice).** Now take a second step on the staircase. You have decided to lose weight and become a healthy version of yourself. You have decided to eat healthily and develop a healthy exercise routine to reach your ideal healthy weight goal **(repeat twice).** Now take another step upward on the staircase. You know that you deserve to live a happy and healthy life. You have the power to change your mind and body. You know that you and your body are unique and respond to healthy eating and exercise habits in a way that is ideal for you. You are aware that you will lose extra pounds soon because nothing is stronger than your willpower **(repeat twice).**

Now with your increased motivation and positivity, take another step on the staircase. Losing weight comes naturally to you. You are very determined and motivated to eat clean and healthy and hitting a gym on regular basis to lose weight and maintain a healthy weight **(repeat twice).** You respect yourself. Your body is your priority **(repeat twice).** You can resist temptations that can become a hurdle in your weight loss journey **(repeat twice).**

Now take another step upwards on a staircase. You are aware that you have your own goals and you do not compare yourself to others **(repeat twice).** You deserve to live a life of fitness and full of energy **(repeat twice).** You find confidence in feeling strong and healthy **(repeat twice).** Losing weight will make you appear vibrant **(repeat twice).**

Now take another step upwards on a staircase. You commit yourself to be your best self. You are willing to give up on habits that were weighing down your weight loss journey. You are a mindful person who is aware of what they eat and why they eat **(repeat twice).** You think before you eat. You will ignore the false messages of hunger. You will differentiate between false hunger and real hunger. You will nourish your body with protein, vegetables and fruits. You will remain hydrated. You love your healthy food and savor every bite you take. Eating healthy and clean food will boost your good mood. You know that your food choices affect not just your body but your mind too. You are willing to be consistent to achieve an optimal mind and body state. You know that your body will reward you for eating right kind of foods.

Now take another step upwards on a staircase. You are becoming mindful of everything you do in life. You are willing to try out new habits that upgrade your lifestyle. You are willing to nourish your body through healthy foods that burn fat and have fewer calories and will assist you in losing excess weight. You know that eating better will make you feel better. You will nourish your body with only important nutrients **(repeat twice).**

Now you will climb the last staircase to reach the small house and you will realize that the more you take care of yourself and maintain balance in your daily routine between healthy meals and exercise, the more positive and strength you will feel.

As you imagine yourself at your desired weight goal you will feel confident, empowered, fit and energetic **(repeat twice).** You will feel that unhealthy habits do not have any control over you **(repeat twice).** You are fully focused on your present self and willing to work and invest in your amazing future self. You are succeeding in your life and you can achieve anything in life you want if you set your eyes on it. Nothing can overwhelm you. You believe in patience and progress.

Now take your moment. Let this feeling of increased motivation and determination speed up your journey of weight loss. Pursuing healthy clean foods and choosing a healthy lifestyle to improve your health and achieve an optimal level of fitness. A surge of positivity flows through your body and you feel free, happy, empowered, and confident more than ever to pursue healthy life choices and continue choosing your health over everything else.

Now bring back your attention to this present moment. Take a deep breath. Inhale deeply and exhale deeply. Again inhale deeply and exhale deeply. And then in a few moments coming back to the here and now with this instinctive new learning in place with balance restored, becoming aware of the room around you and the sounds around you. Feeling revitalized and positive for your future. Now, I am going to count down from ten to one. And as I count ..., you will slowly begin to feel alert, coming back to the present moment and will start opening your eyes slowly. 10... 9…8…7…6…5…4…3…2…and 1. Now begin to stretch and move your arms and legs slowly. Gently and slowly open your eyes, feeling relaxed, positive, peaceful, confident, and alert. Keep on sitting or lying down at your present state for a while to restore your balance. Avoid making any sudden moves and avoid start walking immediately.

Thank you for listening to guided mediation targeted at weight loss. Try to listen to weight loss guided meditation twice a week for attaining better results. For achieving astonishing results combine this guided mediation with given empowering self-affirmations for weight loss. We wish you all the best in your journey of weight loss.

b. Guided Meditation Script for Self-confidence

Timings: 20-25 minutes

Welcome to your hypnosis training session for building self-confidence. This training is specially designed to enable you to develop healthy self-confidence in life. For best results, please give it your full attention and do not listen to it while doing activities where you need to maintain focus.
Now please make sure that you're seated in a comfortable chair, or lying down comfortably at a place where you will be undisturbed for some time. This guided meditation session will take about 20-25 minutes.

(NOTE: USE EYE FACSINATION INDUCTION)

{Sit comfortably in your chair or lay down comfortably in your bed. Make sure your head, neck, shoulders and knees are supported against the back of the chair or a pillow. Now I want you to find some point in your room and stare at it in a position where you are comfortable looking at it. Now keep on staring at that point. Keep staring...Keep Staring. Slowly you will start to notice that the more you stare at the point, the more your eyelids will start to get heavy and you will feel the urge to blink. The more you stare, the more your eyelids will get heavy and the urge to blink will get intense. Now blink your eyes slowly... Now blink again slowly... With each blink, your eyes will become heavy... heavy... so heavy and heavier... that due to this feeling of heaviness it will become difficult for you to keep your eyes open. Now because of this feeling of heaviness in your eyes, you will prefer your eyes to stay closed. Now close your eyes slowly and gently... Very slowly and gently. }

(OR USE HAND AND FINGER SPREADING INDUCTION)

{Now I want you to life up your arm and hand. Place the palm of your hand in front of your face. Make sure you are not wearing any glasses. Your palm should be at least 15 inches away from your face. Your hand fingers should be straight up and a bit above the eye level. Hold your elbow firmly. Now stare at your middle finger and let go of your hold on your elbow. Now keep on staring at your middle finger. Keep Staring. The more you stare at your middle finger the more you will feel that your fingers are starting to spread wider and wider. Now continue staring at your middle finger and you will feel that your hand is slowly pulling in towards your face as your fingers continue to spread. Slowly you will start to notice that the more you stare at the middle finger, your breathing will start to get deeper. And you will notice that the more your eyelids will start to get heavy and you will feel the urge to blink. The more you stare, the more your eyelids will get heavy and the urge to blink will get intense. Now blink your eyes slowly... Now blink again slowly... With each blink, your eyes will become heavy... heavy... so heavy and heavier… that due to this feeling of heaviness it will become difficult for you to keep your eyes open. Now because of this feeling of heaviness in your eyes, you will prefer your eyes to stay closed. Now close your eyes slowly and gently… Very slowly and gently. Now when your palm touches gently front of your face, you will bring your hand down and put in on your lap or belly or put it where ever you feel the comfortable position is for your hand. }

Now that your eyes are closed, put your one hand on your belly and another hand on your chest. As you inhale/breathe in you will feel your belly rising. And when you will exhale you will feel your belly lowering. Take a deep breath. Inhale slowly through your nose and then exhale slowly through your mouth. Feel the air going inside through your nose and feel the air coming outside through your mouth. If it is difficult for you to inhale through your nostrils then inhale through your mouth. Make sure to take a big deep breaths, not short and shallow breaths.

Take three deep breaths more. Inhale and then exhale. Inhale and then exhale. Inhale and then exhale. With every breath, you exhale you become very deeply relaxed. Now tense the muscles in your feet and then relax them slowly. Now tense the muscles in your calves and then relax them slowly. Now tense the muscles in your thighs and then relax them slowly. Now tense the muscles in your hips and then relax them slowly. Feel the relaxation and calmness moving upward from your feet to your calves towards your thighs and moving slowly towards your hips. You will feel nerves in your feet, calves, thighs, and hips deeply relaxing. Now tense the muscles in your belly and then relax them slowly. Now feel the soothing sensation of relaxation slowly moving your belly muscles. Now feel the deep sense of relaxation moving towards your chest. Your breathing will become very deep, gentle, and rhythmic. Now tense the muscles in your shoulders and then relax them slowly. Now this feeling of relaxation will move towards your shoulders and any tension in your shoulder will go away. Now feel this relaxation moving towards your neck slowly relaxing muscles there. Now tense the muscles in your arms and fingers and then relax them slowly. The feeling of relaxation will become deeper and deeper, and your arms, hand, fingers, and tips of fingernails will start to relax. This soothing feeling of relaxation will move towards your forehead. You will feel your eyelids getting relaxed. Now tense you jaw muscles and then relax them slowly. Your jaw muscles will relax and any tightness will be loosened. The feeling of calmness will flow to your cheeks and your entire body will become saturated with the sense of relaxation and calmness. Now gently place your hand over your heart and feel the gentle pressure warmth of your hand on your rising and falling chest. Feel the pulse of your heart. You will notice that any physical sensations of stress that you are holding in your body will be gone.

Now take a deep breath in and deep breath out, this will allow you to clear your mind from the today's events and thoughts. Just like snow wiping from a windscreen and resulting in a clearer sharp view. Any thoughts related to yesterday, today and tomorrow are now in the background of your attention. Your focus is here in the present moment that is filled with deep relaxation. With each deep breath, you take, you feel becoming deeply relaxed and in control of your mind and body by putting unwanted thoughts far away from the present moment. Just feel your breath for a while. When you notice your mind is wandering, bring back your attention to your breathing and feel your breath coming inside and going outside your body again.

And now I will count from ten down to zero. Each count will represent state of deep relaxation, and with each count down you will feel the deep calmness and relaxation in your body getting deeper and deeper. 10... 9…8…7…6…5…4…3…2…and 1… **(Snaps fingers)** Now deep sleep… Take few moments to let those feelings of calmness and relaxation soak you up. Let these feelings rejuvenate your mind and body. Your mind and body are ready to respond positively.

Now imagine yourself walking through a pathway lined with sparkling green magnificent trees and grass. It's a beautiful day to take a walk with the sunshine streaming through the trees, and the blue sky with beautiful white clouds above you. You can feel the soothing softness of grass beneath your feet. Now feel the cool comfortable breeze gently floating around you as you walk and you will notice your body and mind relaxing with each step you take. Hearing the birds chirping beautiful melody from the treetops, you stop a moment to listen to nature's wonders. Reaching out to lean against a tree, you can feel the rough texture of the bark of the tree and the smell of roses in the air. Take few moments to let those feelings of purification, calmness, and relaxation soak you up. Let these feelings rejuvenate your mind, body, and spirit. Your mind, body, and spirit are ready to respond positively.

As you begin walking again, you will see a beautiful meadow filled with different colors of flowers which will instantly give you a surge of positivity. Now take your moment to soak that positivity in. A feeling of peace, confidence, and healing fills you and you will start feeling light, light like a floating feather. A surge of positivity flows through your body and you feel free, happy, calm, and confident more than ever. As you begin walking again, you will see a basket filled with multi-colored sparkling rhinestones. You will notice three balloons attached to the basket sides with the ropes. The first balloon is labeled as FEAR. As you will move to cut the rope of the first balloon to release it in the air, all of your fears will float away just like the balloon will after you will cut its rope. You feel strong and fearless **(repeat twice).** You will feel your confidence and positivity increasing **(repeat twice).** You feel like a person who is not afraid of anything **(repeat twice).** Now the second balloon is labeled as DOUBT, as you will cut the rope of the second balloon all of your doubts will go away. You will feel light and releasing doubt will give you a new perspective and a new awareness. You will become aware of how the weight of uncertainty has been lifted. You feel like a person who is in control of your life **(repeat twice).** You love and respect yourself **(Repeat twice).** You believe in yourself **(Repeat twice).** Now as you continue to cut the rope of the third balloon labeled as STRESS, you will realize that stress has no value. Nothing can stop you from achieving success in your life **(repeat twice).** You will feel ready to conquer the world. Any rejection is not a step backward but a step forward with more motivation to achieve your goal. You know that failure does not exist, only learning does. You are not afraid of criticism. Your mistakes does not define you. You can choose any direction in life. You are a bold, courageous, and confident person who establishes healthy boundaries **(repeat twice).** With your increasing confidence and positive aura, you will attract people and opportunities which will add value and positivity to your life **(repeat twice).** You are worthy of success. You are a confident, and empowered person who is ready to move forward in her life and ready to accomplish her goals like a champion **(repeat twice).** What a feeling …

Now bring back your attention to this present moment. Take a deep breath. Inhale deeply and exhale deeply. Again inhale deeply and exhale deeply. And then in a few moments coming back to the here and now with this instinctive new learning in place with balance restored, becoming aware of the room around you and the sounds around you. Feeling revitalized and positive for your future. Now, I am going to count down from ten to one. And as I count ..., you will slowly begin to feel alert, coming back to the present moment and will start opening your eyes slowly. 10... 9…8…7…6…5…4…3…2…and 1. Now begin to stretch and move your arms and legs slowly. Gently and slowly open your eyes, feeling relaxed, positive, peaceful, confident, and alert. Keep on sitting or lying down at your present state for a while to restore your balance. Avoid making any sudden moves and avoid start walking immediately.

Thank you for listening to guided mediation for increased self-confidence. Try to listen to guided mediation for increased self-confidence every day for attaining better results. For achieving astonishing results combine this guided mediation with given empowering self-affirmations for self-confidence. We wish you all the best in your journey of developing amazing self-confidence.

c. Guided Meditation Script for Body Self-esteem

Timings: 25-30 minutes

Welcome to your guided meditation training session for building good body self-esteem. This training is specially designed to enable you to develop healthy confidence in your body. For best results, please give it your full attention and do not listen to it while doing activities where you need to maintain focus. Now please make sure that you're seated in a comfortable chair, or lying down comfortably at a place where you will be undisturbed for some time. This guided meditation session will take about 25-30 minutes.

(NOTE: USE EYE FACSINATION INDUCTION)

{Sit comfortably in your chair or lay down comfortably in your bed. Make sure your head, neck, shoulders and knees are supported against the back of the chair or a pillow. Now I want you to find some point in your room and stare at it in a position where you are comfortable looking at it. Now keep on staring at that point. Keep staring…Keep Staring. Slowly you will start to notice that the more you stare at the point, the more your eyelids will start to get heavy and you will feel the urge to blink. The more you stare, the more your eyelids will get heavy and the urge to blink will get intense. Now blink your eyes slowly… Now blink again slowly… With each blink, your eyes will become heavy… heavy… so heavy and heavier… that due to this feeling of heaviness it will become difficult for you to keep your eyes open. Now because of this feeling of heaviness in your eyes, you will prefer your eyes to stay closed. Now close your eyes slowly and gently… Very slowly and gently. }

(OR USE HAND AND FINGER SPREADING INDUCTION)

{Now I want you to life up your arm and hand. Place the palm of your hand in front of your face. Make sure you are not wearing any glasses. Your palm should be at least 15 inches away from your face. Your hand fingers should be straight up and a bit above the eye level. Hold your elbow firmly. Now stare at your middle finger and let go of your hold on your elbow. Now keep on staring at your middle finger. Keep Staring. The more you stare at your middle finger the more you will feel that your fingers are starting to spread wider and wider. Now continue staring at your middle finger and you will feel that your hand is slowly pulling in towards your face as your fingers continue to spread. Slowly you will start to notice that the more you stare at the middle finger, your breathing will start to get deeper. And you will notice that the more your eyelids will start to get heavy and you will feel the urge to blink. The more you stare, the more your eyelids will get heavy and the urge to blink will get intense. Now blink your eyes slowly… Now blink again slowly… With each blink, your eyes will become heavy… heavy… so heavy and heavier… that due to this feeling of heaviness it will become difficult for you to keep your eyes open. Now because of this feeling of heaviness in your eyes, you will prefer your eyes to stay closed. Now close your eyes slowly and gently… Very slowly and gently. Now when your palm touches gently front of your face, you will bring your hand down and put in on your lap or belly or put it where ever you feel the comfortable position is for your hand. }

Now that your eyes are closed, put your one hand on your belly and another hand on your chest. As you inhale/breathe in you will feel your belly rising. And when you will exhale you will feel your belly lowering. Take a deep breath. Inhale slowly through your nose and then exhale slowly through your mouth. Feel the air going inside through your nose and feel the air coming outside through your mouth. If it is difficult for you to inhale through your nostrils then inhale through your mouth. Make sure to take a big deep breaths, not short and shallow breaths.

Take three deep breaths more. Inhale and then exhale. Inhale and then exhale. Inhale and then exhale. With every breath, you exhale you become very deeply relaxed. Now tense the muscles in your feet and then relax them slowly. Now tense the muscles in your calves and then relax them slowly. Now tense the muscles in your thighs and then relax them slowly. Now tense the muscles in your hips and then relax them slowly. Feel the relaxation and calmness moving upward from your feet to your calves towards your thighs and moving slowly towards your hips. You will feel nerves in your feet, calves, thighs, and hips deeply relaxing. Now tense the muscles in your belly and then relax them slowly. Now feel the soothing sensation of relaxation slowly moving your belly muscles. Now feel the deep sense of relaxation moving towards your chest. Your breathing will become very deep, gentle, and rhythmic. Now tense the muscles in your shoulders and then relax them slowly. Now this feeling of relaxation will move towards your shoulders and any tension in your shoulder will go away. Now feel this relaxation moving towards your neck slowly relaxing muscles there. Now tense the muscles in your arms and fingers and then relax them slowly. The feeling of relaxation will become deeper and deeper, and your arms, hand, fingers, and tips of fingernails will start to relax. This soothing feeling of relaxation will move towards your forehead. You will feel your eyelids getting relaxed. Now tense you jaw muscles and then relax them slowly. Your jaw muscles will relax and any tightness will be loosened. The feeling of calmness will flow to your cheeks and your entire body will become saturated with the sense of relaxation and calmness. Now gently place your hand over your heart and feel the gentle pressure warmth of your hand on your rising and falling chest. Feel the pulse of your heart. You will notice that any physical sensations of stress that you are holding in your body will be gone.

Now take a deep breath in and deep breath out, this will allow you to clear your mind from the today's events and thoughts. Just like snow wiping from a windscreen and resulting in a clearer sharp view. Any thoughts related to yesterday, today and tomorrow are now in the background of your attention. Your focus is here in the present moment that is filled with deep relaxation. With each deep breath, you take, you feel becoming deeply relaxed and in control of your mind and body by putting unwanted thoughts far away from the present moment. Just feel your breath for a while. When you notice your mind is wandering, bring back your attention to your breathing and feel your breath coming inside and going outside your body again.

And now I will count from ten down to zero. Each count will represent state of deep relaxation, and with each count down you will feel the deep calmness and relaxation in your body getting deeper and deeper. 10... 9…8…7…6…5…4…3…2…and 1… **(Snaps fingers)** Now deep sleep… Take few moments to let those feelings of calmness and relaxation soak you up. Let these feelings rejuvenate your mind and body. Your mind and body are ready to respond positively.

Now imagine yourself walking through a pathway lined with sparkling green magnificent trees and grass. It's a beautiful day to take a walk with the sunshine streaming through the trees, and the blue sky with beautiful white clouds above you. You can feel the soothing softness of grass beneath your feet. Now feel the cool comfortable breeze gently floating around you as you walk and you will notice your body and mind relaxing with each step you take. Hearing the birds chirping beautiful melody from the treetops, you stop a moment to listen to nature's wonders. Reaching out to lean against a tree, you can feel the rough texture of the bark of the tree and the smell of roses in the air. Take few moments to let those feelings of purification, calmness, and relaxation soak you up. Let these feelings rejuvenate your mind, body, and spirit. Your mind, body, and spirit are ready to respond positively.

As you begin walking again, you will see a beautiful meadow filled with different colors of flowers which will instantly give you a surge of positivity. Now take your moment to soak that positivity in. A feeling of peace, confidence, and healing fills you and you will start feeling light, light like a floating feather. A surge of positivity flows through your body and you feel free, happy, calm, and confident more than ever. As you begin walking again, you will see a beautiful large mirror decorated with multi-colored sparkling rhinestones and white gorgeous pearls. As you will get closer to the mirror you will see your amazing self, standing looking in the mirror right at herself. You will realize that your body is an instrument that helps you in achieving daily tasks. You love and respect your body. You are a person who takes care of her body and eats healthy. Your body is a vessel for nurturing and healing. You love your body as it allows you to experience the world around you. Your body is strong and beautiful **(repeat twice)**. Your body is your choice and you are a person who chooses to fuel her body with love **(repeat twice).** Your body is your home. A home that you nurture with love and care. There is no such thing as perfect or ideal body size. You feel perfect, safe, and satisfied in your body **(repeat twice).** You accept and respect your body as it is **(repeat twice).** The more you take care of your body the more your body will be able to assist you in achieving great things. You will feel that that the more trust you place in your body, the more satisfied and confident you will feel in your body. You are your unique self. No one is like you and that is your ultimate power. You reclaim your power and confidence in your body **(repeat twice).**

Now take your moment to soak those feelings of positivity, body confidence, and healthy self-worth in. A feeling of peace, confidence, and healing fills your mind and body and you will start feeling light, light like a floating feather. A surge of positivity flows through your body and you feel free, happy, calm, and self-worthy more than ever.

Now bring back your attention to this present moment. Take a deep breath. Inhale deeply and exhale deeply. Again inhale deeply and exhale deeply. And then in a few moments coming back to the here and now with this instinctive new learning in place with balance restored, becoming aware of the room around you and the sounds around you. Feeling revitalized and positive for your future. Now, I am going to count down from ten to one. And as I count ..., you will slowly begin to feel alert, coming back to the present moment and will start opening your eyes slowly. 10... 9...8...7...6...5...4...3...2...and 1. Now begin to stretch and move your arms and legs slowly. Gently and slowly open your eyes, feeling relaxed, positive, peaceful, confident, and alert. Keep on sitting or lying down at your present state for a while to restore your balance. Avoid making any sudden moves and avoid start walking immediately.

Thank you for listening to guided mediation for increased self-esteem. Try to listen to guided mediation for increased self-esteem every day for attaining better results. . For achieving astonishing results combine this guided mediation with given empowering self-affirmations for body self-esteem. We wish you all the best in your journey of developing positive body self-esteem.

2. Hypnosis Scripts

d. Hypnosis Script for Self-confidence

Timings: 20-25 minutes

Welcome to your hypnosis training session for building self-confidence. This training is specially designed to enable you to develop healthy self-confidence in life. For best results, please give it your full attention and do not listen to it while doing activities where you need to maintain focus.

Now please make sure that you're seated in a comfortable chair, or lying down comfortably at a place where you will be undisturbed for some time. This hypnosis session will take about 20-25 minutes.

(NOTE: USE EYE FACSINATION INDUCTION)

{Sit comfortably in your chair or lay down comfortably in your bed. Make sure your head, neck, shoulders and knees are supported against the back of the chair or a pillow. Now I want you to find some point in your room and stare at it in a position where you are comfortable looking at it. Now keep on staring at that point. Keep staring…Keep Staring. Slowly you will start to notice that the more you stare at the point, the more your eyelids will start to get heavy and you will feel the urge to blink. The more you stare, the more your eyelids will get heavy and the urge to blink will get intense. Now blink your eyes slowly… Now blink again slowly… With each blink, your eyes will become heavy… heavy… so heavy and heavier… that due to this feeling of heaviness it will become difficult for you to keep your eyes open. Now because of this feeling of heaviness in your eyes, you will prefer your eyes to stay closed. Now close your eyes slowly and gently… Very slowly and gently. }

(OR USE HAND AND FINGER SPREADING INDUCTION)

{Now I want you to life up your arm and hand. Place the palm of your hand in front of your face. Make sure you are not wearing any glasses. Your palm should be at least 15 inches away from your face. Your hand fingers should be straight up and a bit above the eye level. Hold your elbow firmly. Now stare at your middle finger and let go of your hold on your elbow. Now keep on staring at your middle finger. Keep Staring. The more you stare at your middle finger the more you will feel that your fingers are starting to spread wider and wider. Now continue staring at your middle finger and you will feel that your hand is slowly pulling in towards your face as your fingers continue to spread. Slowly you will start to notice that the more you stare at the middle finger, your breathing will start to get deeper. And you will notice that the more your eyelids will start to get heavy and you will feel the urge to blink. The more you stare, the more your eyelids will get heavy and the urge to blink will get intense. Now blink your eyes slowly…

Now blink again slowly… With each blink, your eyes will become heavy… heavy… so heavy and heavier… that due to this feeling of heaviness it will become difficult for you to keep your eyes open. Now because of this feeling of heaviness in your eyes, you will prefer your eyes to stay closed. Now close your eyes slowly and gently… Very slowly and gently. Now when your palm touches gently front of your face, you will bring your hand down and put in on your lap or belly or put it where ever you feel the comfortable position is for your hand. }

Now that your eyes are closed, put your one hand on your belly and another hand on your chest. As you inhale/breathe in you will feel your belly rising. And when you will exhale you will feel your belly lowering. Take a deep breath. Inhale slowly through your nose and then exhale slowly through your mouth. Feel the air going inside through your nose and feel the air coming outside through your mouth. If it is difficult for you to inhale through your nostrils then inhale through your mouth. Make sure to take a big deep breaths, not short and shallow breaths.

Take three deep breaths more. Inhale and then exhale. Inhale and then exhale. Inhale and then exhale. With every breath, you exhale you become very deeply relaxed. Now tense the muscles in your feet and then relax them slowly. Now tense the muscles in your calves and then relax them slowly. Now tense the muscles in your thighs and then relax them slowly. Now tense the muscles in your hips and then relax them slowly. Feel the relaxation and calmness moving upward from your feet to your calves towards your thighs and moving slowly towards your hips. You will feel nerves in your feet, calves, thighs, and hips deeply relaxing. Now tense the muscles in your belly and then relax them slowly. Now feel the soothing sensation of relaxation slowly moving your belly muscles. Now feel the deep sense of relaxation moving towards your chest. Your breathing will become very deep, gentle, and rhythmic. Now tense the muscles in your shoulders and then relax them slowly. Now this feeling of relaxation will move towards your shoulders and any tension in your shoulder will go away. Now feel this relaxation moving towards your neck slowly relaxing muscles there. Now tense the muscles in your arms and fingers and then relax them slowly. The feeling of relaxation will become deeper and deeper, and your arms, hand, fingers, and tips of fingernails will start to relax. This soothing feeling of relaxation will move towards your forehead. You will feel your eyelids getting relaxed. Now tense you jaw muscles and then relax them slowly. Your jaw muscles will relax and any tightness will be loosened. The feeling of calmness will flow to your cheeks and your entire body will become saturated with the sense of relaxation and calmness. Now gently place your hand over your heart and feel the gentle pressure warmth of your hand on your rising and falling chest. Feel the pulse of your heart. You will notice that any physical sensations of stress that you are holding in your body will be gone.

Now take a deep breath in and deep breath out, this will allow you to clear your mind from the today's events and thoughts. Just like snow wiping from a windscreen and resulting in a clearer sharp view. Any thoughts related to yesterday, today and tomorrow are now in the background of your attention. Your focus is here in the present moment that is filled with deep relaxation. With each deep breath, you take, you feel becoming deeply relaxed and in control of your mind and body by putting unwanted thoughts far away from the present moment. Just feel your breath for a while. When you notice your mind is wandering, bring back your attention to your breathing and feel your breath coming inside and going outside your body again.

And now I will count from ten down to zero. Each count will represent state of deep relaxation, and with each count down you will feel the deep calmness and relaxation in your body getting deeper and deeper. 10... 9...8...7...6...5...4...3...2...and 1... **(Snaps fingers)** Now deep sleep... Take few moments to let those feelings of calmness and relaxation soak you up. Let these feelings rejuvenate your mind and body. Your mind and body are ready to respond positively.

You are feeling strong and fearless. You will feel your confidence and positivity increasing **(repeat twice).** You feel like a person who is in control of your life. You love and respect yourself **(Repeat twice).** You believe in yourself **(Repeat twice).** You accept yourself as you are. You will be more kind towards yourself. You forgive yourself and your past. Your past does not define you who you are and your self-worth. You will not stress yourself over things that you can't control. You will live in the present moment. You do not worry about your future because you are giving your best already. Nothing can stop you from achieving success in your life. You are ready to conquer the world. Any rejection is not a step backward but a step forward with more motivation to achieve your goal. You are not afraid of anything. You are a non-judgmental person who is mindful. You are a logical person who lives in the present and love and accept yourself as you are. You are a bold, courageous, and confident person who establishes health boundaries **(repeat twice).** With your increasing confidence and positive aura, you will attract people and opportunities which will add value and positivity to your life **(repeat twice).** What a feeling ...

Now take your moment to soak that positivity in. A feeling of peace, confidence, and healing fills you and you will start feeling light, light like a floating feather. A surge of positivity flows through your body and you feel free, happy, calm, and confident more than ever.

Now bring back your attention to this present moment. Take a deep breath. Inhale deeply and exhale deeply. Again inhale deeply and exhale deeply. And then in a few moments coming back to the here and now with this instinctive new learning in place with balance restored, becoming aware of the room around you and the sounds around you. Feeling revitalized and positive for your future. Now, I am going to count down from ten to one. And as I count ..., you will slowly begin to feel alert, coming back to the present moment and will start opening your eyes slowly. 10... 9…8…7…6…5…4…3…2…and 1. Now begin to stretch and move your arms and legs slowly. Gently and slowly open your eyes, feeling relaxed, positive, peaceful, confident, and alert. Keep on sitting or lying down at your present state for a while to restore your balance. Avoid making any sudden moves and avoid start walking immediately.

Thank you for listening to self-hypnosis for increased self-confidence. Try to listen to self-hypnosis for increased self-confidence every day for attaining better results. . For achieving astonishing results combine this guided mediation with given empowering self-affirmations for self-confidence. We wish you all the best in your journey of developing amazing self-confidence.

e. Hypnosis Script for Body Self-Esteem

Timings: 25-30 minutes

Welcome to your hypnosis training session for building good body self-esteem. This training is specially designed to enable you to develop healthy confidence in your body. For best results, please give it your full attention and do not listen to it while doing activities where you need to maintain focus. Now please make sure that you're seated in a comfortable chair, or lying down comfortably at a place where you will be undisturbed for some time. This hypnosis session will take about 25-30 minutes.

(NOTE: USE EYE FACSINATION INDUCTION)

{Sit comfortably in your chair or lay down comfortably in your bed. Make sure your head, neck, shoulders and knees are supported against the back of the chair or a pillow. Now I want you to find some point in your room and stare at it in a position where you are comfortable looking at it. Now keep on staring at that point. Keep staring…Keep Staring. Slowly you will start to notice that the more you stare at the point, the more your eyelids will start to get heavy and you will feel the urge to blink. The more you stare, the more your eyelids will get heavy and the urge to blink will get intense. Now blink your eyes slowly… Now blink again slowly… With each blink, your eyes will become heavy… heavy… so heavy and heavier… that due to this feeling of heaviness it will become difficult for you to keep your eyes open. Now because of this feeling of heaviness in your eyes, you will prefer your eyes to stay closed. Now close your eyes slowly and gently… Very slowly and gently. }

(OR USE HAND AND FINGER SPREADING INDUCTION)

{Now I want you to life up your arm and hand. Place the palm of your hand in front of your face. Make sure you are not wearing any glasses. Your palm should be at least 15 inches away from your face. Your hand fingers should be straight up and a bit above the eye level. Hold your elbow firmly. Now stare at your middle finger and let go of your hold on your elbow. Now keep on staring at your middle finger. Keep Staring. The more you stare at your middle finger the more you will feel that your fingers are starting to spread wider and wider. Now continue staring at your middle finger and you will feel that your hand is slowly pulling in towards your face as your fingers continue to spread. Slowly you will start to notice that the more you stare at the middle finger, your breathing will start to get deeper. And you will notice that the more your eyelids will start to get heavy and you will feel the urge to blink. The more you stare, the more your eyelids will get heavy and the urge to blink will get intense. Now blink your eyes slowly... Now blink again slowly... With each blink, your eyes will become heavy... heavy... so heavy and heavier... that due to this feeling of heaviness it will become difficult for you to keep your eyes open. Now because of this feeling of heaviness in your eyes, you will prefer your eyes to stay closed. Now close your eyes slowly and gently... Very slowly and gently. Now when your palm touches gently front of your face, you will bring your hand down and put in on your lap or belly or put it where ever you feel the comfortable position is for your hand. }

Now that your eyes are closed, put your one hand on your belly and another hand on your chest. As you inhale/breathe in you will feel your belly rising. And when you will exhale you will feel your belly lowering. Take a deep breath. Inhale slowly through your nose and then exhale slowly through your mouth. Feel the air going inside through your nose and feel the air coming outside through your mouth. If it is difficult for you to inhale through your nostrils then inhale through your mouth. Make sure to take a big deep breaths, not short and shallow breaths.

Take three deep breaths more. Inhale and then exhale. Inhale and then exhale. Inhale and then exhale. With every breath, you exhale you become very deeply relaxed. Now tense the muscles in your feet and then relax them slowly. Now tense the muscles in your calves and then relax them slowly. Now tense the muscles in your thighs and then relax them slowly. Now tense the muscles in your hips and then relax them slowly. Feel the relaxation and calmness moving upward from your feet to your calves towards your thighs and moving slowly towards your hips. You will feel nerves in your feet, calves, thighs, and hips deeply relaxing. Now tense the muscles in your belly and then relax them slowly. Now feel the soothing sensation of relaxation slowly moving your belly muscles. Now feel the deep sense of relaxation moving towards your chest. Your breathing will become very deep, gentle, and rhythmic. Now tense the muscles in your shoulders and then relax them slowly. Now this feeling of relaxation will move towards your shoulders and any tension in your shoulder will go away. Now feel this relaxation moving towards your neck slowly relaxing muscles there. Now tense the muscles in your arms and fingers and then relax them slowly. The feeling of relaxation will become deeper and deeper, and your arms, hand, fingers, and tips of fingernails will start to relax. This soothing feeling of relaxation will move towards your forehead. You will feel your eyelids getting relaxed. Now tense you jaw muscles and then relax them slowly. Your jaw muscles will relax and any tightness will be loosened. The feeling of calmness will flow to your cheeks and your entire body will become saturated with the sense of relaxation and calmness. Now gently place your hand over your heart and feel the gentle pressure warmth of your hand on your rising and falling chest. Feel the pulse of your heart. You will notice that any physical sensations of stress that you are holding in your body will be gone.

And now I will count from ten down to zero. Each count will represent state of deep relaxation, and with each count down you will feel the deep calmness and relaxation in your body getting deeper and deeper. 10... 9…8…7…6…5…4…3…2…and 1… **(Snaps fingers)** Now deep sleep… Take few moments to let those feelings of calmness and relaxation soak you up. Let these feelings rejuvenate your mind and body. Your mind and body are ready to respond positively.

Now think of all the body part you just scanned with the feeling of relaxation. Bring a feeling of gratitude towards your body. How grateful you are for your body and its parts that help to perform different tasks. Notice your feeling of respect and affection increasing for your body. Now put your hand on your heart. Feel the warmth of your hand on your chest and say to yourself. *I love and respect myself. I accept myself as I am. I will be more kind towards myself* **(repeat twice).** *I forgive myself and my past. My past does not define me who I am. I will not stress myself over things that I can't control. I will live in the present moment.*

Now take a deep breath…

Now say to yourself that it is okay to make mistakes. *I forgive my mistakes and mistakes of others.* Forgiving yourself and others will give you a sense of peace. Feel this feeling of peace travel down from the back of your neck to your spine. Take your moment. Let this feeling of peace and relaxation rejuvenate you. Now when you are ready bring your attention back to your breathing and in the present moment.

Now take a deep breath in and deep breath out, this will allow you to clear your mind from the today's events and thoughts. Just like snow wiping from a windscreen and resulting in a clearer sharp view. Any thoughts related to yesterday, today and tomorrow are now in the background of your attention. Your focus is here in the present moment that is filled with deep relaxation. With each deep breath, you take, you feel becoming deeply relaxed and in control of your mind and body by putting unwanted thoughts far away from the present moment. Just feel your breath for a while. When you notice your mind is wandering, bring back your attention to your breathing and feel your breath coming inside and going outside your body again.

And now I will count from ten down to zero. Each count will represent state of deep relaxation, and with each count down you will feel the deep calmness and relaxation in your body getting deeper and deeper. Take few moments to let those feelings of calmness and relaxation soak you up. Let these feelings rejuvenate your mind and body. Your mind and body are ready to respond positively.

You love and respect your body. You are a person who takes care of her body and eats healthy. Your body is a vessel for nurturing and healing. Your body is an instrument that helps you in achieving daily tasks. You love your body as it allows you to experience the world around you. Your body is strong and beautiful **(repeat twice)**. Your body is your choice and you are a person who chooses to fuel her body with love **(repeat twice).** Your body is your home. A home that you nurture with love and care. There is no such thing as perfect or ideal body size. You feel perfect, protected, and satisfied in your body **(repeat twice).** You accept and respect your body as it is **(repeat twice).** The more you take care of your body the more your body will be able to assist you in achieving great things. You will feel that that the more trust you place in your body, the more satisfied and confident you will feel in your body. You reclaim your power and confidence in your body **(repeat twice).**

Now take your moment to soak those feelings of positivity, body confidence, and healthy self-worth in. A feeling of peace, confidence, and healing fills your mind and body and you will start feeling light, light like a floating feather. A surge of positivity flows through your body and you feel free, happy, calm, and self-worthy more than ever.

Now bring back your attention to this present moment. Take a deep breath. Inhale deeply and exhale deeply. Again inhale deeply and exhale deeply. And then in a few moments coming back to the here and now with this instinctive new learning in place with balance restored, becoming aware of the room around you and the sounds around you. Feeling revitalized and positive for your future. Now, I am going to count down from ten to one. And as I count ..., you will slowly begin to feel alert, coming back to the present moment and will start opening your eyes slowly. 10... 9…8…7…6…5…4…3…2…and 1. Now begin to stretch and move your arms and legs slowly. Gently and slowly open your eyes, feeling relaxed, positive, peaceful, confident, and alert. Keep on sitting or lying down at your present state for a while to restore your balance. Avoid making any sudden moves and avoid start walking immediately.

Thank you for listening to self-hypnosis for increased self-esteem. Try to listen to self-hypnosis for increased self-esteem every day for attaining better results. For achieving astonishing results combine this self-hypnosis guide with given empowering self-affirmations for body self-esteem. We wish you all the best in your journey of developing positive body self-esteem.

f. Hypnosis Script for overcoming Food Addiction

Timings: 25-30 minutes

Welcome to your hypnosis training session for overcoming Food Addiction. This training is specially designed to enable you to develop a healthy eating habit. For best results, please give it your full attention and do not listen to it while doing activities where you need to maintain focus.

Now please make sure that you're seated in a comfortable chair, or lying down comfortably at a place where you will be undisturbed for some time. This hypnosis session will take about 25-30 minutes.

(NOTE: USE EYE FACSINATION INDUCTION)

{Sit comfortably in your chair or lay down comfortably in your bed. Make sure your head, neck, shoulders and knees are supported against the back of the chair or a pillow. Now I want you to find some point in your room and stare at it in a position where you are comfortable looking at it. Now keep on staring at that point. Keep staring…Keep Staring. Slowly you will start to notice that the more you stare at the point, the more your eyelids will start to get heavy and you will feel the urge to blink. The more you stare, the more your eyelids will get heavy and the urge to blink will get intense. Now blink your eyes slowly… Now blink again slowly… With each blink, your eyes will become heavy… heavy… so heavy and heavier… that due to this feeling of heaviness it will become difficult for you to keep your eyes open. Now because of this feeling of heaviness in your eyes, you will prefer your eyes to stay closed. Now close your eyes slowly and gently… Very slowly and gently. }

(OR USE HAND AND FINGER SPREADING INDUCTION)

{Now I want you to life up your arm and hand. Place the palm of your hand in front of your face. Make sure you are not wearing any glasses. Your palm should be at least 15 inches away from your face. Your hand fingers should be straight up and a bit above the eye level. Hold your elbow firmly. Now stare at your middle finger and let go of your hold on your elbow. Now keep on staring at your middle finger. Keep Staring. The more you stare at your middle finger the more you will feel that your fingers are starting to spread wider and wider. Now continue staring at your middle finger and you will feel that your hand is slowly pulling in towards your face as your fingers continue to spread. Slowly you will start to notice that the more you stare at the middle finger, your breathing will start to get deeper. And you will notice that the more your eyelids will start to get heavy and you will feel the urge to blink. The more you stare, the more your eyelids will get heavy and the urge to blink will get intense. Now blink your eyes slowly... Now blink again slowly... With each blink, your eyes will become heavy... heavy... so heavy and heavier... that due to this feeling of heaviness it will become difficult for you to keep your eyes open. Now because of this feeling of heaviness in your eyes, you will prefer your eyes to stay closed. Now close your eyes slowly and gently... Very slowly and gently. Now when your palm touches gently front of your face, you will bring your hand down and put in on your lap or belly or put it where ever you feel the comfortable position is for your hand. }

Now that your eyes are closed, put your one hand on your belly and another hand on your chest. As you inhale/breathe in you will feel your belly rising. And when you will exhale you will feel your belly lowering. Take a deep breath. Inhale slowly through your nose and then exhale slowly through your mouth. Feel the air going inside through your nose and feel the air coming outside through your mouth. If it is difficult for you to inhale through your nostrils then inhale through your mouth. Make sure to take a big deep breaths, not short and shallow breaths.

Take three deep breaths more. Inhale and then exhale. Inhale and then exhale. Inhale and then exhale. With every breath, you exhale you become very deeply relaxed. Now tense the muscles in your feet and then relax them slowly. Now tense the muscles in your calves and then relax them slowly. Now tense the muscles in your thighs and then relax them slowly. Now tense the muscles in your hips and then relax them slowly. Feel the relaxation and calmness moving upward from your feet to your calves towards your thighs and moving slowly towards your hips. You will feel nerves in your feet, calves, thighs, and hips deeply relaxing. Now tense the muscles in your belly and then relax them slowly. Now feel the soothing sensation of relaxation slowly moving your belly muscles. Now feel the deep sense of relaxation moving towards your chest. Your breathing will become very deep, gentle, and rhythmic. Now tense the muscles in your shoulders and then relax them slowly. Now this feeling of relaxation will move towards your shoulders and any tension in your shoulder will go away. Now feel this relaxation moving towards your neck slowly relaxing muscles there. Now tense the muscles in your arms and fingers and then relax them slowly. The feeling of relaxation will become deeper and deeper, and your arms, hand, fingers, and tips of fingernails will start to relax. This soothing feeling of relaxation will move towards your forehead. You will feel your eyelids getting relaxed. Now tense you jaw muscles and then relax them slowly. Your jaw muscles will relax and any tightness will be loosened. The feeling of calmness will flow to your cheeks and your entire body will become saturated with the sense of relaxation and calmness. Now gently place your hand over your heart and feel the gentle pressure warmth of your hand on your rising and falling chest. Feel the pulse of your heart. You will notice that any physical sensations of stress that you are holding in your body will be gone.

Now take a deep breath in and deep breath out, this will allow you to clear your mind from the today's events and thoughts. Just like snow wiping from a windscreen and resulting in a clearer sharp view. Any thoughts related to yesterday, today and tomorrow are now in the background of your attention. Your focus is here in the present moment that is filled with deep relaxation. With each deep breath, you take, you feel becoming deeply relaxed and in control of your mind and body by putting unwanted thoughts far away from the present moment. Just feel your breath for a while. When you notice your mind is wandering, bring back your attention to your breathing and feel your breath coming inside and going outside your body again.

And now I will count from ten down to zero. Each count will represent state of deep relaxation, and with each count down you will feel the deep calmness and relaxation in your body getting deeper and deeper. 10... 9…8…7…6…5…4…3…2…and 1… **(Snaps fingers)** Now deep sleep… Take few moments to let those feelings of calmness and relaxation soak you up. Let these feelings rejuvenate your mind and body. Your mind and body are ready to respond positively.

You are a person who respects her body. You fuel your body with healthy meals. You are fully aware of your body's needs and eat only when you are hungry **(repeat twice)**. You only prefer to eat healthy meals and healthy snacks **(repeat twice).** You are very motivated to not give in to any kind of food addiction. You know that junk food is not your first option and you are very motivated to start eating healthy. You are in control of your impulses **(repeat twice).** You believe in a healthy lifestyle **(repeat twice).** From this very moment, you will start nurturing and healthily healing your body through healthy meals and proper exercise. Eating healthy and clean food will boost your good mood. You will improve your eating habits with proper meal planning, exercise routine, and confidence in yourself. You will only eat healthy to fuel your body. You will eat slowly and consciously savoring your food. You are proud of your decision of eating healthy **repeat twice).** You will be proud of how you are making your body healthier, full of strength and energy. Your willpower is stronger than you're unhealthy and timeless food cravings **(repeat twice).** You are fully in control of your life including your food cravings and problems. You trust and care for yourself **(repeat twice).** You are a person who believes in lifestyle and self-transformation **(repeat twice).**

Now take your moment. Let this feeling of increased motivation to overcome food addiction and starting a healthy lifestyle to improve your health that fills your body and mind with calmness. A surge of positivity flows through your body and you feel free, happy, determined, and confident more than ever to pursue healthy life choices and continue choosing your health over everything else.

Now bring back your attention to this present moment. Take a deep breath. Inhale deeply and exhale deeply. Again inhale deeply and exhale deeply. And then in a few moments coming back to the here and now with this instinctive new learning in place with balance restored, becoming aware of the room around you and the sounds around you. Feeling revitalized and positive for your future. Now, I am going to count down from ten to one. And as I count ..., you will slowly begin to feel alert, coming back to the present moment and will start opening your eyes slowly. 10... 9...8...7...6...5...4...3...2...and 1. Now begin to stretch and move your arms and legs slowly. Gently and slowly open your eyes, feeling relaxed, positive, peaceful, confident, and alert. Keep on sitting or lying down at your present state for a while to restore your balance. Avoid making any sudden moves and avoid start walking immediately.

Thank you for listening to self-hypnosis for overcoming food addiction. Try to listen to self-hypnosis for overcoming food addiction twice a week for attaining better results. For achieving astonishing results combine this self-hypnosis guide mediation with given empowering self-affirmations for overcoming food addiction. We wish you all the best in your journey to develop healthy eating habits and exercise routine.

g. Hypnosis Script for Overcoming Emotional Eating

Timings: 25-30 minutes

Welcome to your hypnosis training session for overcoming Emotional Eating. This training is specially designed to enable you to develop healthy habits to deal with your emotions and feelings instead of eating them out. For best results, please give it your full attention and do not listen to it while doing activities where you need to maintain focus.

Now please make sure that you're seated in a comfortable chair, or lying down comfortably at a place where you will be undisturbed for some time. This hypnosis session will take about 25-30 minutes.

(NOTE: USE EYE FACSINATION INDUCTION)

{Sit comfortably in your chair or lay down comfortably in your bed. Make sure your head, neck, shoulders and knees are supported against the back of the chair or a pillow. Now I want you to find some point in your room and stare at it in a position where you are comfortable looking at it. Now keep on staring at that point. Keep staring...Keep Staring. Slowly you will start to notice that the more you stare at the point, the more your eyelids will start to get heavy and you will feel the urge to blink. The more you stare, the more your eyelids will get heavy and the urge to blink will get intense. Now blink your eyes slowly...

Now blink again slowly... With each blink, your eyes will become heavy... heavy... so heavy and heavier... that due to this feeling of heaviness it will become difficult for you to keep your eyes open. Now because of this feeling of heaviness in your eyes, you will prefer your eyes to stay closed. Now close your eyes slowly and gently... Very slowly and gently. }

(OR USE HAND AND FINGER SPREADING INDUCTION)

{Now I want you to life up your arm and hand. Place the palm of your hand in front of your face. Make sure you are not wearing any glasses. Your palm should be at least 15 inches away from your face. Your hand fingers should be straight up and a bit above the eye level. Hold your elbow firmly. Now stare at your middle finger and let go of your hold on your elbow. Now keep on staring at your middle finger. Keep Staring. The more you stare at your middle finger the more you will feel that your fingers are starting to spread wider and wider. Now continue staring at your middle finger and you will feel that your hand is slowly pulling in towards your face as your fingers continue to spread. Slowly you will start to notice that the more you stare at the middle finger, your breathing will start to get deeper. And you will notice that the more your eyelids will start to get heavy and you will feel the urge to blink. The more you stare, the more your eyelids will get heavy and the urge to blink will get intense. Now blink your eyes slowly... Now blink again slowly... With each blink, your eyes will become heavy... heavy... so heavy and heavier... that due to this feeling of heaviness it will become difficult for you to keep your eyes open. Now because of this feeling of heaviness in your eyes, you will prefer your eyes to stay closed. Now close your eyes slowly and gently... Very slowly and gently. Now when your palm touches gently front of your face, you will bring your hand down and put in on your lap or belly or put it where ever you feel the comfortable position is for your hand. }

Now that your eyes are closed, put your one hand on your belly and another hand on your chest. As you inhale/breathe in you will feel your belly rising. And when you will exhale you will feel your belly lowering. Take a deep breath. Inhale slowly through your nose and then exhale slowly through your mouth. Feel the air going inside through your nose and feel the air coming outside through your mouth. If it is difficult for you to inhale through your nostrils then inhale through your mouth. Make sure to take a big deep breaths, not short and shallow breaths.

Take three deep breaths more. Inhale and then exhale. Inhale and then exhale. Inhale and then exhale. With every breath, you exhale you become very deeply relaxed. Now tense the muscles in your feet and then relax them slowly. Now tense the muscles in your calves and then relax them slowly. Now tense the muscles in your thighs and then relax them slowly. Now tense the muscles in your hips and then relax them slowly. Feel the relaxation and calmness moving upward from your feet to your calves towards your thighs and moving slowly towards your hips. You will feel nerves in your feet, calves, thighs, and hips deeply relaxing. Now tense the muscles in your belly and then relax them slowly. Now feel the soothing sensation of relaxation slowly moving your belly muscles. Now feel the deep sense of relaxation moving towards your chest. Your breathing will become very deep, gentle, and rhythmic. Now tense the muscles in your shoulders and then relax them slowly. Now this feeling of relaxation will move towards your shoulders and any tension in your shoulder will go away. Now feel this relaxation moving towards your neck slowly relaxing muscles there. Now tense the muscles in your arms and fingers and then relax them slowly. The feeling of relaxation will become deeper and deeper, and your arms, hand, fingers, and tips of fingernails will start to relax. This soothing feeling of relaxation will move towards your forehead. You will feel your eyelids getting relaxed. Now tense you jaw muscles and then relax them slowly. Your jaw muscles will relax and any tightness will be loosened. The feeling of calmness will flow to your cheeks and your entire body will become saturated with the sense of relaxation and calmness. Now gently place your hand over your heart and feel the gentle pressure warmth of your hand on your rising and falling chest. Feel the pulse of your heart. You will notice that any physical sensations of stress that you are holding in your body will be gone.

Now take a deep breath in and deep breath out, this will allow you to clear your mind from the today's events and thoughts. Just like snow wiping from a windscreen and resulting in a clearer sharp view. Any thoughts related to yesterday, today and tomorrow are now in the background of your attention. Your focus is here in the present moment that is filled with deep relaxation. With each deep breath, you take, you feel becoming deeply relaxed and in control of your mind and body by putting unwanted thoughts far away from the present moment. Just feel your breath for a while. When you notice your mind is wandering, bring back your attention to your breathing and feel your breath coming inside and going outside your body again.

And now I will count from ten down to zero. Each count will represent state of deep relaxation, and with each count down you will feel the deep calmness and relaxation in your body getting deeper and deeper. 10... 9…8…7…6…5…4…3…2…and 1… **(Snaps fingers)** Now deep sleep… Take few moments to let those feelings of calmness and relaxation soak you up. Let these feelings rejuvenate your mind and body. Your mind and body are ready to respond positively.

You are a person who is highly self-aware of herself **(repeat twice).** You know that emotional eating is not a solution to your stress and anxiety. You know that emotional eating will not solve your problems. You are the kind of person who deals with stress and anxiety in a productive way rather than chunking on food. You are a responsible person who takes her health very seriously **(repeat twice).** You prefer to have a healthy relationship with food instead of an emotional relationship. You are strong enough to not let your anxious impulses get carried away into emotional eating. You have control over your emotions **(repeat twice).** You plan to deal with your pent-up emotions healthily **(repeat twice).** You are very motivated to deal with your problems that create stress and anxiety in a productive way instead of indulging in emotional eating. You are a person who knows that eating and emotional comfort are separate **(repeat twice).** You are mindful of why you eat and when you eat **(repeat twice).** You are the master of your thoughts **(repeat twice).** Your emotions are not your boss. You are the boss of your emotions. Your actions are not influenced by your emotions **(repeat twice).** You are the one who is fully in control of your actions. You are a person who eats only healthy food to fuel your body and not your emotions. Eating healthy and clean food will boost your good mood and regulate your positive emotions.

Now take your moment. Let this feeling of increased motivation stop emotional eating and dealing with your problems in a healthy way that fills your body and mind with calmness. A surge of positivity flows through your body and you feel free, happy, determined, and confident more than ever to pursue healthy life choices and productive problem-solving and continue choosing your healthy self over everything else. Now bring back your attention to this present moment. Take a deep breath. Inhale deeply and exhale deeply. Again inhale deeply and exhale deeply. And then in a few moments coming back to the here and now with this instinctive new learning in place with balance restored, becoming aware of the room around you and the sounds around you. Feeling revitalized and positive for your future. Now, I am going to count down from ten to one. And as I count ..., you will slowly begin to feel alert, coming back to the present moment and will start opening your eyes slowly. 10... 9…8…7…6…5…4…3…2…and 1. Now begin to stretch and move your arms and legs slowly. Gently and slowly open your eyes, feeling relaxed, positive, peaceful, confident, and alert. Keep on sitting or lying down at your present state for a while to restore your balance. Avoid making any sudden moves and avoid start walking immediately.

Thank you for listening to self-hypnosis for overcoming emotional eating. Try to listen to self-hypnosis for overcoming emotional eating twice a week for attaining better results. For achieving astonishing results combine this self-hypnosis guide mediation with given empowering self-affirmations for overcoming emotional eating. We wish you all the best in your journey to develop healthy eating habits and dealing with your problems productively.

h. Hypnosis Script for overcoming Sugar Cravings

Timings: 35-40 minutes

Welcome to your hypnosis training session for overcoming Sugar Cravings. This training is specially designed to enable you to develop a motivation to overcome sugar cravings and choosing clean food. For best results, please give it your full attention and do not listen to it while doing activities where you need to maintain focus.

Now please make sure that you're seated in a comfortable chair, or lying down comfortably at a place where you will be undisturbed for some time. This hypnosis session will take about 35-40 minutes.

(NOTE: USE EYE FACSINATION INDUCTION)

{Sit comfortably in your chair or lay down comfortably in your bed. Make sure your head, neck, shoulders and knees are supported against the back of the chair or a pillow. Now I want you to find some point in your room and stare at it in a position where you are comfortable looking at it. Now keep on staring at that point. Keep staring…Keep Staring. Slowly you will start to notice that the more you stare at the point, the more your eyelids will start to get heavy and you will feel the urge to blink. The more you stare, the more your eyelids will get heavy and the urge to blink will get intense. Now blink your eyes slowly… Now blink again slowly… With each blink, your eyes will become heavy… heavy… so heavy and heavier… that due to this feeling of heaviness it will become difficult for you to keep your eyes open. Now because of this feeling of heaviness in your eyes, you will prefer your eyes to stay closed. Now close your eyes slowly and gently… Very slowly and gently. }

(OR USE HAND AND FINGER SPREADING INDUCTION)

{Now I want you to life up your arm and hand. Place the palm of your hand in front of your face. Make sure you are not wearing any glasses. Your palm should be at least 15 inches away from your face. Your hand fingers should be straight up and a bit above the eye level. Hold your elbow firmly. Now stare at your middle finger and let go of your hold on your elbow. Now keep on staring at your middle finger. Keep Staring. The more you stare at your middle finger the more you will feel that your fingers are starting to spread wider and wider. Now continue staring at your middle finger and you will feel that your hand is slowly pulling in towards your face as your fingers continue to spread. Slowly you will start to notice that the more you stare at the middle finger, your breathing will start to get deeper. And you will notice that the more your eyelids will start to get heavy and you will feel the urge to blink. The more you stare, the more your eyelids will get heavy and the urge to blink will get intense. Now blink your eyes slowly… Now blink again slowly… With each blink, your eyes will become heavy… heavy… so heavy and heavier… that due to this feeling of heaviness it will become difficult for you to keep your eyes open.

Now because of this feeling of heaviness in your eyes, you will prefer your eyes to stay closed. Now close your eyes slowly and gently… Very slowly and gently. Now when your palm touches gently front of your face, you will bring your hand down and put in on your lap or belly or put it where ever you feel the comfortable position is for your hand. }

Now that your eyes are closed, put your one hand on your belly and another hand on your chest. As you inhale/breathe in you will feel your belly rising. And when you will exhale you will feel your belly lowering. Take a deep breath. Inhale slowly through your nose and then exhale slowly through your mouth. Feel the air going inside through your nose and feel the air coming outside through your mouth. If it is difficult for you to inhale through your nostrils then inhale through your mouth. Make sure to take a big deep breaths, not short and shallow breaths.

Take three deep breaths more. Inhale and then exhale. Inhale and then exhale. Inhale and then exhale. With every breath, you exhale you become very deeply relaxed. Now tense the muscles in your feet and then relax them slowly. Now tense the muscles in your calves and then relax them slowly. Now tense the muscles in your thighs and then relax them slowly. Now tense the muscles in your hips and then relax them slowly. Feel the relaxation and calmness moving upward from your feet to your calves towards your thighs and moving slowly towards your hips. You will feel nerves in your feet, calves, thighs, and hips deeply relaxing. Now tense the muscles in your belly and then relax them slowly. Now feel the soothing sensation of relaxation slowly moving your belly muscles. Now feel the deep sense of relaxation moving towards your chest. Your breathing will become very deep, gentle, and rhythmic. Now tense the muscles in your shoulders and then relax them slowly. Now this feeling of relaxation will move towards your shoulders and any tension in your shoulder will go away. Now feel this relaxation moving towards your neck slowly relaxing muscles there. Now tense the muscles in your arms and fingers and then relax them slowly. The feeling of relaxation will become deeper and deeper, and your arms, hand, fingers, and tips of fingernails will start to relax. This soothing feeling of relaxation will move towards your forehead. You will feel your eyelids getting relaxed. Now tense you jaw muscles and then relax them slowly. Your jaw muscles will relax and any tightness will be loosened. The feeling of calmness will flow to your cheeks and your entire body will become saturated with the sense of relaxation and calmness. Now gently place your hand over your heart and feel the gentle pressure warmth of your hand on your rising and falling chest. Feel the pulse of your heart. You will notice that any physical sensations of stress that you are holding in your body will be gone.

Now take a deep breath in and deep breath out, this will allow you to clear your mind from the today's events and thoughts. Just like snow wiping from a windscreen and resulting in a clearer sharp view. Any thoughts related to yesterday, today and tomorrow are now in the background of your attention. Your focus is here in the present moment that is filled with deep relaxation. With each deep breath, you take, you feel becoming deeply relaxed and in control of your mind and body by putting unwanted thoughts far away from the present moment. Just feel your breath for a while. When you notice your mind is wandering, bring back your attention to your breathing and feel your breath coming inside and going outside your body again.

And now I will count from ten down to zero. Each count will represent state of deep relaxation, and with each count down you will feel the deep calmness and relaxation in your body getting deeper and deeper. 10... 9...8...7...6...5...4...3...2...and 1... **(Snaps fingers)** Now deep sleep... Take few moments to let those feelings of calmness and relaxation soak you up. Let these feelings rejuvenate your mind and body. Your mind and body are ready to respond positively.

You are a person who is in control of choosing what to eat. You deserve to be healthy **(repeat twice).** You have control over your impulses and can resist sugar cravings. Today you decide to let go of your sugar cravings. Quitting sugary food comes easy to you. You are stronger than your sugar cravings. Sugar does not have control over you. You can resist candies, chocolates, and all kinds of sugary stuff. Sugar does not have the power to entice you. You believe in yourself and are fully in control of stopping your sugar cravings **(repeat twice).** You love taking care of your body **(repeat twice).** You prefer eating healthy fruits and vegetables every time. Every day you will choose to eat whole foods instead of sugary food. You are in control of your mind, body, and spirit. You are in full control of your appetite and food choices **(repeat twice).** You have power and control over your life and your body. You do not need sugar. You feel liberated from sugar cravings. You respect your body **(repeat twice).** You take care of your body **(repeat twice).** You don't need sugar to live a happy life **(repeat twice).** You are powerful enough to easily deal with whatever comes into your life. You are determined to let go of your sugar cravings. Your willpower is strong enough to resist the urge to eat sugary foods. You are not tempted to eat sugar. You choose to buy healthy food. You choose to eat healthy and clean food **(repeat twice).** Eating healthy and clean food will boost your good mood. You do not need sugar to boost your mood. You accept sugar-free eating as your priority lifestyle. You only seek out food that makes you healthy. You have the power to politely decline sugary food when it is offered to you. You do not resent not eating sugary food. You decline sugary food in total peace and satisfaction **(repeat twice).** You have the power to turn down sugar **(repeat twice).** You believe in transforming your life into a positive healthier one. You are stronger than any kind of cravings **(repeat twice).**

Now take your moment. Let this feeling of increased motivation and determination stop craving sugar and pursuing healthy clean foods and choosing a healthy lifestyle to improve your health and fills your body and mind with calmness. A surge of positivity flows through your body and you feel free, happy, determined, and confident more than ever to pursue healthy life choices and continue choosing your health over everything else.

Now bring back your attention to this present moment. Take a deep breath. Inhale deeply and exhale deeply. Again inhale deeply and exhale deeply. And then in a few moments coming back to the here and now with this instinctive new learning in place with balance restored, becoming aware of the room around you and the sounds around you. Feeling revitalized and positive for your future. Now, I am going to count down from ten to one. And as I count ..., you will slowly begin to feel alert, coming back to the present moment and will start opening your eyes slowly. 10... 9…8…7…6…5…4…3…2…and 1. Now begin to stretch and move your arms and legs slowly. Gently and slowly open your eyes, feeling relaxed, positive, peaceful, confident, and alert. Keep on sitting or lying down at your present state for a while to restore your balance. Avoid making any sudden moves and avoid start walking immediately.

Thank you for listening to self-hypnosis for overcoming sugar cravings. Try to listen to self-hypnosis for overcoming sugar cravings thrice a week for attaining better results. For achieving astonishing results combine this self-hypnosis guide mediation with given empowering self-affirmations for overcoming sugar cravings. We wish you all the best in your journey to develop clean and healthy eating habits.

i. Hypnosis Script for extreme Fat Burning

Timings: 30-40 minutes

Welcome to your hypnosis training session for extreme Fat Burning for weight loss. This training is specially designed to enable you to achieve a healthy lean body. For best results, please give it your full attention and do not listen to it while doing activities where you need to maintain focus.

Now please make sure that you're seated in a comfortable chair, or lying down comfortably at a place where you will be undisturbed for some time. This hypnosis session will take about 30-40 minutes.

(NOTE: USE EYE FACSINATION INDUCTION)

{Sit comfortably in your chair or lay down comfortably in your bed. Make sure your head, neck, shoulders and knees are supported against the back of the chair or a pillow. Now I want you to find some point in your room and stare at it in a position where you are comfortable looking at it. Now keep on staring at that point. Keep staring…Keep Staring. Slowly you will start to notice that the more you stare at the point, the more your eyelids will start to get heavy and you will feel the urge to blink. The more you stare, the more your eyelids will get heavy and the urge to blink will get intense. Now blink your eyes slowly… Now blink again slowly… With each blink, your eyes will become heavy… heavy… so heavy and heavier… that due to this feeling of heaviness it will become difficult for you to keep your eyes open. Now because of this feeling of heaviness in your eyes, you will prefer your eyes to stay closed. Now close your eyes slowly and gently… Very slowly and gently. }

(OR USE HAND AND FINGER SPREADING INDUCTION)

{Now I want you to life up your arm and hand. Place the palm of your hand in front of your face. Make sure you are not wearing any glasses. Your palm should be at least 15 inches away from your face. Your hand fingers should be straight up and a bit above the eye level. Hold your elbow firmly. Now stare at your middle finger and let go of your hold on your elbow. Now keep on staring at your middle finger. Keep Staring. The more you stare at your middle finger the more you will feel that your fingers are starting to spread wider and wider. Now continue staring at your middle finger and you will feel that your hand is slowly pulling in towards your face as your fingers continue to spread. Slowly you will start to notice that the more you stare at the middle finger, your breathing will start to get deeper. And you will notice that the more your eyelids will start to get heavy and you will feel the urge to blink. The more you stare, the more your eyelids will get heavy and the urge to blink will get intense. Now blink your eyes slowly… Now blink again slowly… With each blink, your eyes will become heavy… heavy… so heavy and heavier… that due to this feeling of heaviness it will become difficult for you to keep your eyes open. Now because of this feeling of heaviness in your eyes, you will prefer your eyes to stay closed. Now close your eyes slowly and gently… Very slowly and gently. Now when your palm touches gently front of your face, you will bring your hand down and put in on your lap or belly or put it where ever you feel the comfortable position is for your hand. }

Now that your eyes are closed, put your one hand on your belly and another hand on your chest. As you inhale/breathe in you will feel your belly rising. And when you will exhale you will feel your belly lowering. Take a deep breath. Inhale slowly through your nose and then exhale slowly through your mouth. Feel the air going inside through your nose and feel the air coming outside through your mouth. If it is difficult for you to inhale through your nostrils then inhale through your mouth. Make sure to take a big deep breaths, not short and shallow breaths.

Take three deep breaths more. Inhale and then exhale. Inhale and then exhale. Inhale and then exhale. With every breath, you exhale you become very deeply relaxed. Now tense the muscles in your feet and then relax them slowly. Now tense the muscles in your calves and then relax them slowly. Now tense the muscles in your thighs and then relax them slowly. Now tense the muscles in your hips and then relax them slowly. Feel the relaxation and calmness moving upward from your feet to your calves towards your thighs and moving slowly towards your hips. You will feel nerves in your feet, calves, thighs, and hips deeply relaxing. Now tense the muscles in your belly and then relax them slowly. Now feel the soothing sensation of relaxation slowly moving your belly muscles. Now feel the deep sense of relaxation moving towards your chest. Your breathing will become very deep, gentle, and rhythmic. Now tense the muscles in your shoulders and then relax them slowly. Now this feeling of relaxation will move towards your shoulders and any tension in your shoulder will go away. Now feel this relaxation moving towards your neck slowly relaxing muscles there. Now tense the muscles in your arms and fingers and then relax them slowly. The feeling of relaxation will become deeper and deeper, and your arms, hand, fingers, and tips of fingernails will start to relax. This soothing feeling of relaxation will move towards your forehead. You will feel your eyelids getting relaxed. Now tense you jaw muscles and then relax them slowly. Your jaw muscles will relax and any tightness will be loosened. The feeling of calmness will flow to your cheeks and your entire body will become saturated with the sense of relaxation and calmness. Now gently place your hand over your heart and feel the gentle pressure warmth of your hand on your rising and falling chest. Feel the pulse of your heart. You will notice that any physical sensations of stress that you are holding in your body will be gone.

Now take a deep breath in and deep breath out, this will allow you to clear your mind from the today's events and thoughts. Just like snow wiping from a windscreen and resulting in a clearer sharp view. Any thoughts related to yesterday, today and tomorrow are now in the background of your attention. Your focus is here in the present moment that is filled with deep relaxation. With each deep breath, you take, you feel becoming deeply relaxed and in control of your mind and body by putting unwanted thoughts far away from the present moment. Just feel your breath for a while. When you notice your mind is wandering, bring back your attention to your breathing and feel your breath coming inside and going outside your body again.

And now I will count from ten down to zero. Each count will represent state of deep relaxation, and with each count down you will feel the deep calmness and relaxation in your body getting deeper and deeper. 10... 9…8…7…6…5…4…3…2…and 1… **(Snaps fingers)** Now deep sleep… Take few moments to let those feelings of calmness and relaxation soak you up. Let these feelings rejuvenate your mind and body. Your mind and body are ready to respond positively.

You are in control of your life choices. You choose to eat healthily and develop a healthy exercise routine to burn and lose excess fat from your body **(repeat twice).** You deserve a lean body with a healthy fat ratio **(repeat twice).** You and your body are unique and respond to healthy eating and exercise habits in a way that is ideal for you. Losing fat comes naturally to you. You are very determined and motivated to eat clean and healthy and hitting a gym on regular basis to get a lean body **(repeat twice).** You enjoy working out. You believe that exercise will impact your life in a positive way and hasten your journey of fat loss. You are willing to find new creative ways to move your body in ways that will assist you in burning excessive fat in your body and achieving your ideal desired weight and lean body. You plan to eat low fat foods that will help you to develop lean body. Eating healthy clean foods and exercising regularly will boost your good mood. You are capable of maintaining disciple, self-control, and self-mastery over yourself **(repeat twice).** You can resist temptations that come in your fat loss journey **(repeat twice).** You are determined to make your metabolism runs at its optimal level **(repeat twice).** You have your own goals and you do not compare yourself to others **(repeat twice).** You deserve to live a life of fitness and full of energy **(repeat twice).** You find confidence in feeling strong and healthy **(repeat twice).** Every day you will follow your healthy meal plans and exercise routine. and you will notice that the more you follow your healthy meal plans and exercise routine, more relax, more refreshed and more energized you will feel. Take few moments to let that energized and feeling of refreshment soak you up and motivates you. Today and every coming day will be the best and amazing day of your life **(repeat twice).** You will feel productive and optimistic. You are powerful enough to make everything drift in the way you want **(repeat twice).**

Now take your moment. Let this feeling of increased motivation and determination speed up your journey of extreme fat loss. Pursuing healthy clean foods and choosing a healthy lifestyle to improve your health and achieve an optimal level of fitness. A surge of positivity flows through your body and you feel free, happy, determined, and confident more than ever to pursue healthy life choices.

Now bring back your attention to this present moment. Take a deep breath. Inhale deeply and exhale deeply. Again inhale deeply and exhale deeply. And then in a few moments coming back to the here and now with this instinctive new learning in place with balance restored, becoming aware of the room around you and the sounds around you. Feeling revitalized and positive for your future. Now, I am going to count down from ten to one. And as I count ..., you will slowly begin to feel alert, coming back to the present moment and will start opening your eyes slowly. 10... 9…8…7…6…5…4…3…2…and 1. Now begin to stretch and move your arms and legs slowly. Gently and slowly open your eyes, feeling relaxed, positive, peaceful, confident, and alert. Keep on sitting or lying down at your present state for a while to restore your balance. Avoid making any sudden moves and avoid start walking immediately.

Thank you for listening to self-hypnosis for extreme fat burning. Try to listen to self-hypnosis for extreme fat burning twice a week for attaining better results. For achieving astonishing results combine this self-hypnosis guide mediation with given empowering self-affirmations for extreme fat burning. We wish you all the best in your journey to develop healthy eating habits, exercise routine and boosting your metabolism to its optimal potential.

3. Self-affirmations

j. Self-affirmations for Weight loss

Note: Repeat self-affirmations daily for maximum impact.

1. I am kind to my body.
2. I am very motivated and determined to lose weight.
3. I am becoming open to new positive thoughts and actions.
4. I am very determined to bring a positive and healthy change to my lifestyle.
5. I am going after what I want.
6. I am in control of my life choices.
7. Nothing can stop me to achieve what I set my mind to.
8. I have decided to lose weight and become a healthy version of myself.
9. I have decided to eat healthily and develop a healthy exercise routine to reach my ideal healthy weight goal.
10. I deserve to live a happy and healthy life.
11. My and my body is unique and responds to healthy eating and exercise habits in a way that is ideal for me.
12. I will lose extra pounds soon because nothing is stronger than my willpower.
13. Losing weight comes naturally and easy to me.
14. I have the power to change my mind and body.
15. I am very determined and motivated to eat clean and healthy and hitting a gym on regular basis to lose weight and maintain a healthy weight.
16. I respect you.
17. My body is my priority.
18. I can resist temptations that can become a hurdle in my weight loss journey.
19. I have my own goals and I do not compare myself to others.
20. I deserve to live a life of fitness and full of energy.
21. I find confidence in feeling strong and healthy.
22. Losing weight will make me appear vibrant.
23. I commit myself to be my best self.
24. I am willing to give up on habits that were weighing down my weight loss journey.

25. I am a mindful person who is aware of what I eat and why I eat.
26. I think before I eat.
27. I love my healthy food and savor every bite I take.
28. I know that my food choices affect not just my body but my mind too.
29. I am willing to be consistent to achieve an optimal mind and body state.
30. I am becoming mindful of everything I do in my life.
31. I am willing to try out new habits that will upgrade my lifestyle.
32. I am willing to nourish my body through healthy foods that burn fat and have fewer calories and assist me in losing excessive weight.
33. The more I take care of myself and maintain balance in my daily routine between healthy meals and exercise, the more positive and strength I will feel.
34. I feel confident, empowered, fit, and energetic.
35. Unhealthy habits do not have any control over me.
36. I am fully focused on becoming a better version of my present self.
37. I am willing to work and invest in my amazing future self.
38. I am succeeding in my life.
39. I can achieve anything in life I want if I set my eyes on it.
40. I believe in wellness lifestyle.
41. I choose wellness lifestyle for myself.

k. Self-affirmations for Self-confidence

Note: Repeat self-affirmations daily for maximum impact.

1. I feeling strong and fearless.
2. I feel my confidence and positivity increasing day by day.
3. I feel like a person who is in control of my life.
4. I love and respect myself.
5. I believe in myself.
6. Nothing can stop me from achieving success in my life.
7. I am ready to conquer the world.
8. Any rejection is not a step backward but a step forward with more motivation to achieve my goal.

9. I am not afraid of anything.

10. I am a bold, courageous, and confident person.

11. I believe in establishing healthy boundaries for myself and others.

12. I have increasing confidence and a positive aura.

13. I attract people and opportunities which add value and positivity to my life.

14. I accept myself as I am.

15. I will be more kind towards myself.

16. I forgive myself and my past. My past does not define me who I am.

17. I will not stress myself over things that I can't control.

18. I will live in the present moment.

I. Self-affirmations for body self-esteem

Note: Repeat self-affirmations daily for maximum impact.

1. I love and respect my body.
2. I am a person who takes care of her body and eats healthy.
3. My body is a vessel for nurturing and healing.
4. My body is an instrument that helps me in achieving daily tasks.
5. I love my body as it allows me to experience the world around me.
6. My body is strong and beautiful.
7. My body is my choice.
8. I am a person who chooses to fuel her body with love.
9. My body is my home.
10. I nurture my body with love and care.
11. There is no such thing as perfect or ideal body size.
12. I feel perfect, protected, and satisfied in my body.
13. I am my priority.
14. I accept and respect my body as it is.
15. The more I take care of my body the more my body will be able to assist me in achieving great things.
16. The more trust I place in my body, the more satisfied and confident I feel in my body.
17. I reclaim my power and confidence in my body.

18. I accept myself as I am.
19. I will be more kind towards myself. I forgive myself and my past.
20. My past does not define me who I am.
21. I will not stress myself over things that I can't control.
22. I will live in the present moment.

m. Self-affirmations for overcoming food addiction

Note: Repeat self-affirmations daily for maximum impact.

1. I am a person who respects her body.
2. I fuel my body with healthy meals.
3. I am fully aware of my body's needs.
4. I eat only when I am hungry.
5. I only prefer to eat healthy meals and healthy snacks.
6. I am very motivated to not give in to any kind of food addiction.
7. Junk food is not my first option.
8. I am very motivated to start eating healthy.
9. I am in control of my impulses.
10. I believe in a healthy lifestyle.
11. I nurture and healthily heal my body through healthy meals and proper exercise.
12. I am improving my eating habits with proper meal planning, exercise routine.
13. I have confidence in myself and I trust my ability to give up food addiction.
14. I will only eat healthy to fuel my body.
15. I will eat slowly and chew my food mindfully.
16. I love how eating healthy makes me feel.
17. I will eat consciously and will savor my food.
18. I am proud of my decision of eating healthy.
19. I am proud of how I am making my body healthier, full of strength and energy.
20. My willpower is stronger than my unhealthy and timeless food cravings.
21. I am fully in control of my life and food choices.
22. I am fully in control of my food cravings and problems.
23. I trust and care for myself.

24. I am a person who believes in lifestyle and self-transformation.

n. Self-affirmations for overcoming emotional eating

Note: Repeat self-affirmations daily for maximum impact.

1. I am a person who is highly self-aware of herself.
2. I know that emotional eating is not a solution to my stress and anxiety.
3. I know that emotional eating will not solve my problems.
4. I am the kind of person who deals with stress and anxiety in a productive way rather than chunking on food.
5. I am a responsible person who takes her health very seriously.
6. I prefer to have a healthy relationship with food instead of an emotional relationship.
7. I am strong enough to not let my anxious impulses get carried away into emotional eating.
8. I have control over my emotions.
9. I plan to deal with my pent-up emotions healthily.
10. Emotional eating is not my catharsis.
11. I am very motivated to deal with my problems that create stress and anxiety in a productive way instead of indulging in emotional eating.
12. I am a person who knows that eating and emotional comfort are separate.
13. I am mindful of why I eat and when I eat and how I eat.
14. I am the master of my thoughts.
15. My emotions are not my boss.
16. I am the boss of my emotions.
17. My actions are not influenced by my emotions.
18. I am the one who is fully in control of my actions.
19. I am a person who eats only healthy food to fuel my body and not my emotions.
20. Nothing can overwhelm me.

o. Self-affirmations for overcoming sugar cravings

Note: Repeat self-affirmations daily for maximum impact.

1. I decided to give up sugar.
2. I am in control of choosing what to eat.
3. I deserve to be healthy.
4. I have control over my impulses and can resist sugar cravings.
5. I decide to let go of my sugar cravings.
6. Quitting sugary food comes easy to me.
7. I am stronger than my sugar cravings.
8. Sugar does not have control over me.
9. I can resist candies, chocolates, and all kinds of sugary stuff.
10. Sugar does not have the power to entice me.
11. I believe in myself and am fully in control of stopping my sugar cravings.
12. I love taking care of my body.
13. I prefer eating healthy fruits and vegetables every time.
14. Every day I will choose to eat whole foods instead of sugary food.
15. I am in control of my mind, body, and spirit.
16. I am in full control of my appetite and food choices.
17. I have power and control over my life and my body.
18. I do not need sugar.
19. I feel liberated from sugar cravings.
20. I respect my body.
21. I enjoy eating healthy food.
22. I take care of my body.
23. I do not need sugar to live a happy life.
24. I am powerful enough to easily deal with whatever comes into my life.
25. I am determined to let go of my sugar cravings.
26. My willpower is strong enough to resist the urge to eat sugary foods.
27. I am not tempted to eat sugar.
28. I choose to buy healthy food.
29. I choose to eat healthy and clean food.
30. I accept sugar-free eating as my priority lifestyle.

31. I only seek out food that makes me healthy.
32. I have the power to politely decline sugary foods when they are being offered to me.
33. I do not resent not eating sugary food.
34. I decline sugary food in total peace and satisfaction.
35. I have the power to turn down sugar.
36. I believe in transforming my life into a positive healthier one.
37. I am stronger than any kind of cravings.

p. Self-affirmations for extreme fat loss

Note: Repeat self-affirmations daily for maximum impact.

1. My mind and body are responding positively.
2. I am in control of my life choices.
3. I choose to eat healthily.
4. I choose to develop a healthy exercise routine to burn and lose excess fat from my body.
5. I deserve a lean body with a healthy fat ratio.
6. I and my body is unique and respond to healthy eating and exercise habits in a way that is ideal for me.
7. I enjoy working out.
8. Exercise will release my stress.
9. Exercise will impact me positively.
10. Losing fat comes naturally and easy to me.
11. I am very determined and motivated to eat clean and healthy.
12. I am very determined to hit a gym on regular basis to get a lean body.
13. I am willing to find new creative ways to move my body in ways that will assist me in burning excessive fat in my body.
14. I am very determined to achieve my ideal desired weight and lean body.
15. I am capable of maintaining disciple, self-control, and self-mastery over myself.
16. I can resist temptations that come in my fat loss journey.
17. I am determined to make my metabolism runs at its optimal level.
18. I have my own goals.
19. I believe in patience and progress.
20. I am creating lean and healthy body that I deserve.

21. I do not compare myself to other people.

22. I deserve to live a life of fitness and full of energy.

23. I feel confident and empowered in feeling strong and healthy.

24. I am very motivated to speed up my journey of extreme fat loss.

25. I am pursuing healthy clean foods.

26. I am choosing a healthy lifestyle to improve my health and achieve an optimal level of fitness.

4. EXPLANATION OF SCRIPTS' PARTS

Guided Meditation Script for Weight Loss (TITLE)

INTRODUCTION AND NARRATION PART

Welcome to your Guided Meditation training session for weight loss. This training is specially designed to enable you to achieve a healthy body, develop healthy eating habits, eating clean and exercise regularly. For best results, please give it your full attention and do not listen to it while doing activities where you need to maintain focus.

TIME LIMIT INDICATION PART

Now please make sure that you're seated in a comfortable chair, or lying down comfortably at a place where you will be undisturbed for some time. This guided meditation session will take about 40-50 minutes.

SETTING PART

Sit comfortably in your chair or lay down comfortably in your bed. Make sure your head, neck, shoulders and knees are supported against the back of the chair or a pillow.

EYE FASCINATION INDUCTION

(NOTE: you can also use hand and finger spreading induction BUT using one induction regularly puts a person in hypnosis state early and easily. it is called LAW OF REPETITION which is a basic science behind hypnosis procedures. I have added hand and finger spreading induction TOO. You can use it as you desire in between scripts.)

(NOTE: USE EYE FACSINATION INDUCTION)

{Now I want you to find some point in your room and stare at it in a position where you are comfortable looking at it. Now keep on staring at that point. Keep staring…Keep Staring. Slowly you will start to notice that the more you stare at the point, the more your eyelids will start to get heavy and you will feel the urge to blink. The more you stare, the more your eyelids will get heavy and the urge to blink will get intense. Now blink your eyes slowly… Now blink again slowly… With each blink, your eyes will become heavy… heavy… so heavy and heavier… that due to this feeling of heaviness it will become difficult for you to keep your eyes open. Now because of this feeling of heaviness in your eyes, you will prefer your eyes to stay closed. Now close your eyes slowly and gently… Very slowly and gently. }

(OR USE HAND AND FINGER SPREADING INDUCTION)

{Now I want you to life up your arm and hand. Place the palm of your hand in front of your face. Make sure you are not wearing any glasses. Your palm should be at least 15 inches away from your face. Your hand fingers should be straight up and a bit above the eye level. Hold your elbow firmly. Now stare at your middle finger and let go of your hold on your elbow. Now keep on staring at your middle finger. Keep Staring. The more you stare at your middle finger the more you will feel that your fingers are starting to spread wider and wider. Now continue staring at your middle finger and you will feel that your hand is slowly pulling in towards your face as your fingers continue to spread. Slowly you will start to notice that the more you stare at the middle finger, your breathing will start to get deeper. And you will notice that the more your eyelids will start to get heavy and you will feel the urge to blink. The more you stare, the more your eyelids will get heavy and the urge to blink will get intense. Now blink your eyes slowly… Now blink again slowly… With each blink, your eyes will become heavy… heavy… so heavy and heavier… that due to this feeling of heaviness it will become difficult for you to keep your eyes open. Now because of this feeling of heaviness in your eyes, you will prefer your eyes to stay closed. Now close your eyes slowly and gently… Very slowly and gently. Now when your palm touches gently front of your face, you will bring your hand down and put in on your lap or belly or put it where ever you feel the comfortable position is for your hand. }

DEEP BREATHING

Now that your eyes are closed, put your one hand on your belly and another hand on your chest. As you inhale/breathe in you will feel your belly rising. And when you will exhale you will feel your belly lowering. Take a deep breath. Inhale slowly through your nose and then exhale slowly through your mouth. Feel the air going inside through your nose and feel the air coming outside through your mouth. If it is difficult for you to inhale through your nostrils then inhale through your mouth. Make sure to take a big deep breaths, not short and shallow breaths.

PROGRESSIVE MUSCLE RELAXATION FOR INDUCTION

Take three deep breaths more. Inhale and then exhale. Inhale and then exhale. Inhale and then exhale. With every breath, you exhale you become very deeply relaxed. Now tense the muscles in your feet and then relax them slowly. Now tense the muscles in your calves and then relax them slowly. Now tense the muscles in your thighs and then relax them slowly. Now tense the muscles in your hips and then relax them slowly. Feel the relaxation and calmness moving upward from your feet to your calves towards your thighs and moving slowly towards your hips. You will feel nerves in your feet, calves, thighs, and hips deeply relaxing. Now tense the muscles in your belly and then relax them slowly. Now feel the soothing sensation of relaxation slowly moving your belly muscles. Now feel the deep sense of relaxation moving towards your chest. Your breathing will become very deep, gentle, and rhythmic. Now tense the muscles in your shoulders and then relax them slowly. Now this feeling of relaxation will move towards your shoulders and any tension in your shoulder will go away. Now feel this relaxation moving towards your neck slowly relaxing muscles there. Now tense the muscles in your arms and fingers and then relax them slowly. The feeling of relaxation will become deeper and deeper, and your arms, hand, fingers, and tips of fingernails will start to relax. This soothing feeling of relaxation will move towards your forehead. You will feel your eyelids getting relaxed. Now tense you jaw muscles and then relax them slowly. Your jaw muscles will relax and any tightness will be loosened. The feeling of calmness will flow to your cheeks and your entire body will become saturated with the sense of relaxation and calmness. Now gently place your hand over your heart and feel the gentle pressure warmth of your hand on your rising and falling chest. Feel the pulse of your heart. You will notice that any physical sensations of stress that you are holding in your body will be gone.

DEEPENING TECHNIQUE FOR INDUCTION

Now take a deep breath in and deep breath out, this will allow you to clear your mind from the today's events and thoughts. Just like snow wiping from a windscreen and resulting in a clearer sharp view. Any thoughts related to yesterday, today and tomorrow are now in the background of your attention. Your focus is here in the present moment that is filled with deep relaxation. With each deep breath, you take, you feel becoming deeply relaxed and in control of your mind and body by putting unwanted thoughts far away from the present moment. Just feel your breath for a while. When you notice your mind is wandering, bring back your attention to your breathing and feel your breath coming inside and going outside your body again.

And now I will count from ten down to zero. Each count will represent state of deep relaxation, and with each count down you will feel the deep calmness and relaxation in your body getting deeper and deeper. 10... 9…8…7…6…5…4…3…2…and 1… **(Snaps fingers)** Now deep sleep… Take few moments to let those feelings of calmness and relaxation soak you up. Let these feelings rejuvenate your mind and body. Your mind and body are ready to respond positively.

Guided IMAGERY and MEDITATION FOR SUGGESTIONS

Now imagine yourself walking through a pathway lined with sparkling green magnificent trees and grass. It's a beautiful day to take a walk with the sunshine streaming through the trees, and the blue sky with beautiful white clouds above you. You can feel the soothing softness of grass beneath your feet. Now feel the cool comfortable breeze gently floating around you as you walk and you will notice your body and mind relaxing with each step you take. Hearing the birds chirping beautiful melody from the treetops, you stop a moment to listen to nature's wonders. Reaching out to lean against a tree, you can feel the rough texture of the bark of the tree and the smell of roses in the air. Take few moments to let those feelings of purification, calmness, and relaxation soak you up. Let these feelings rejuvenate your mind, body, and spirit. Your mind, body, and spirit are ready to respond positively. Now begin walking again and you will notice a small house located at the top of a long beautiful spiral staircase, with sides covered from green branches. The color of green branches will fill you with a soothing feeling of coolness and peace. Now continue walking towards that beautiful staircase. A feeling of calmness, relaxation will take over you. Now visualize the staircase as your pathway towards reaching your goal weight. Each step that you will take on this staircase will bring you closer to your desired weight goal.

Now stand at the 1st staircase and you will notice that you are becoming very motivated and determined to lose weight. You are becoming open to new positive thoughts and actions. You are very determined to bring a positive and healthy change to your lifestyle. You are going after what you want. You are in control of your life choices **(repeat twice).** Nothing can stop you from what you set your mind to **(repeat twice).** Now take a second step on the staircase. You have decided to lose weight and become a healthy version of yourself. You have decided to eat healthily and develop a healthy exercise routine to reach your ideal healthy weight goal **(repeat twice).** Now take another step upward on the staircase. You know that you deserve to live a happy and healthy life. You have the power to change your mind and body. You know that you and your body are unique and respond to healthy eating and exercise habits in a way that is ideal for you. You are aware that you will lose extra pounds soon because nothing is stronger than your willpower **(repeat twice).**

Now with your increased motivation and positivity, take another step on the staircase. Losing weight comes naturally to you. You are very determined and motivated to eat clean and healthy and hitting a gym on regular basis to lose weight and maintain a healthy weight **(repeat twice).** You respect yourself. Your body is your priority **(repeat twice).** You can resist temptations that can become a hurdle in your weight loss journey **(repeat twice).**

Now take another step upwards on a staircase. You are aware that you have your own goals and you do not compare yourself to others **(repeat twice).** You deserve to live a life of fitness and full of energy **(repeat twice).** You find confidence in feeling strong and healthy **(repeat twice).** Losing weight will make you appear vibrant **(repeat twice).**

Now take another step upwards on a staircase. You commit yourself to be your best self. You are willing to give up on habits that were weighing down your weight loss journey. You are a mindful person who is aware of what they eat and why they eat **(repeat twice).** You think before you eat. You will ignore the false messages of hunger. You will differentiate between false hunger and real hunger. You will nourish your body with protein, vegetables and fruits. You will remain hydrated. You love your healthy food and savor every bite you take. Eating healthy and clean food will boost your good mood. You know that your food choices affect not just your body but your mind too. You are willing to be consistent to achieve an optimal mind and body state. You know that your body will reward you for eating right kind of foods.

Now take another step upwards on a staircase. You are becoming mindful of everything you do in life. You are willing to try out new habits that upgrade your lifestyle. You are willing to nourish your body through healthy foods that burn fat and have fewer calories and will assist you in losing excess weight. You know that eating better will make you feel better. You will nourish your body with only important nutrients **(repeat twice).**

Now you will climb the last staircase to reach the small house and you will realize that the more you take care of yourself and maintain balance in your daily routine between healthy meals and exercise, the more positive and strength you will feel.

As you imagine yourself at your desired weight goal you will feel confident, empowered, fit and energetic **(repeat twice).** You will feel that unhealthy habits do not have any control over you **(repeat twice).** You are fully focused on your present self and willing to work and invest in your amazing future self. You are succeeding in your life and you can achieve anything in life you want if you set your eyes on it. Nothing can overwhelm you. You believe in patience and progress.

Now take your moment. Let this feeling of increased motivation and determination speed up your journey of weight loss. Pursuing healthy clean foods and choosing a healthy lifestyle to improve your health and achieve an optimal level of fitness. A surge of positivity flows through your body and you feel free, happy, empowered, and confident more than ever to pursue healthy life choices and continue choosing your health over everything else.

WAKING UP PART

Now bring back your attention to this present moment. Take a deep breath. Inhale deeply and exhale deeply. Again inhale deeply and exhale deeply. And then in a few moments coming back to the here and now with this instinctive new learning in place with balance restored, becoming aware of the room around you and the sounds around you. Feeling revitalized and positive for your future. Now, I am going to count down from ten to one. And as I count ..., you will slowly begin to feel alert, coming back to the present moment and will start opening your eyes slowly. 10... 9…8…7…6…5…4…3…2…and 1. Now begin to stretch and move your arms and legs slowly. Gently and slowly open your eyes, feeling relaxed, positive, peaceful, confident, and alert. Keep on sitting or lying down at your present state for a while to restore your balance. Avoid making any sudden moves and avoid start walking immediately.

RECOMMEDATION FOR USING SELF-AFFIRMATIONS (VERY IMPORTANT IN CASE OF SELF-HYPNOSIS)

Thank you for listening to guided mediation targeted at weight loss. Try to listen to weight loss guided meditation twice a week for attaining better results. For achieving astonishing results combine this guided mediation with given empowering self-affirmations for weight loss. We wish you all the best in your journey of weight loss.

Extreme Weight Loss Hypnosis For Women: Affirmations & Guided Meditations For Rapid Fat Burn, Mindfulness & Healthy Eating Habits + Overcoming Food Addiction

(Hypnotic Gastric Band)

Table of Contents

Introduction:

Hypnotherapy is a method of treatment in which a hypnotist offers some suggestions to a person for a desirable behavioural change. It works when there is focused attention and an altered state of mind. A person under hypnosis may subconsciously absorb all the communication that a hypnotherapist does. The critical mind of a person is lower down through the workload of messages and the change occurs because hypnotic induction allows a person to accept the suggestions for change and able to alter the core beliefs that might limit helpful actions. Through this natural treatment method, research evidence recently boosts the effectiveness of hypnotherapy in managing headaches, pain during invasive dental and other surgical processes, managing anxiety, stress, low mood, confidence building, weight loss and much more.

Hypnosis and weight loss have been explored with the help of several clinical experiments. The efficacy of clinical hypnosis has been established for the assurance of fruitful outcomes for overall health. A variety of medical and mental health disorders are now dealt with with the help of different techniques that hypnosis proposed. Typically for weight loss, hypnosis has been shown improvement in self-control, seeking lower body mass and resolving one's emotional conflicts. Eating problems i.e. excessive or restricting are both harmful for proper weight and women tend to be the victim of eating disorders more often than men however body image shatters in both genders equally. One of the potential factors behind the development of unhealthy weight gain and relevant issues is emotional instability.

Other options to manage weight include surgical procedures and therapeutic interventions. Fasting, chakra balancing, aromatherapy, Tai Chi, nutritional therapy, endoscopic procedures, injections, exercise and yoga are some of the commonly heard solutions. These procedures are time taking, short-term relievers and temporary with greater costs for an average person. There are painful consequences sometimes and it is almost impossible to maintain the benefits from these methods in the long term. Years of follow-up and constant effort are required for ideal weight management. Moderate weight loss goals and slow achievement is always considered more stable than the fastest quick fix. The opposite alternative of all these discussed quick fixers is a form of hypnosis called gastric band hypnosis.

Gastric band hypnosis works directly on the human subconscious mind. The suggestions are given in a way that induces a belief that a tight gastric band is tied around the stomach. It is a traditional concept of surgery through the band at the upper part of the stomach that limits food intake and consumption on daily basis without any alternative thought. The physical band encouraged weight loss but came with undeniably uncontrollable complications. This leads to modern hypnosis to create the experience of the band in imagination. We are what we believe, once we believe that we can eat lesser and healthy.

To accompany weight loss, other techniques are as follows:

Neuro-linguistic programming (NLP) is an approach that elaborates the methodology of communication that directs human beings to take action through a source of their preferred representational learning style through which they speak and listen and perceive sensory information with the help of five senses. One of them is dominant for an individual. The metaphors, expressions and images, sounds, textures that people understand and learn through are some of the ways to integrate verbal communication in hypnotic suggestions. The NLP suggestions even work strongly when the hypnotic state is induced. This is not a directly observed method to bring change in someone but even more influential with access directly to the subconscious.

Affirmations are very frequently combined with hypnotic suggestions for behavioural change. These are positive statements customized to strengthen the beliefs about whatever we want to achieve in life. They work one by one and enable us to modify our action accordingly. Hypnotic inductions facilitate the path of these affirmations to the human mind where we realize our competencies and efficiency. The work that we do is mostly regulated by the beliefs that we affirm ourselves since childhood. The unfortunate bundle of them are irrational, counterproductive, negative and damaging. To compensate for the persistent loss, affirmations are sent through hypnosis and change becomes faster.

Meditations are stress-managing exercises. Meditation is a practice that silently makes the stress levels down to earth. The meditation provides the surface for other similar opportunities to explore. The opportunities positively influence the mind and body to open up for wellbeing. It is guided through meditations and mindfulness exercises that focus is the road to success. The focus is enhanced when hypnosis is induced. It is predicted that the hypnotic state along with meditations smoothly shifts the human being into a fitness-oriented mindset. The connection of mind and body is essential for mind and body psychotherapies to function.

Eating habits and lifestyle guidelines are usually recommended in the shape of hypnotic suggestions for relapse prevention and triggers management. There are some specific triggers emotional, cognitive or behavioural for people that can cause binge eating and unhealthy food picking which is a disaster for the acquired success in weight loss and fat burning journey.

The purpose of the selection of given series of hypnotic scripts is to create a sequential stepwise combination of short, easy to understand non-invasive, pain-free and long-term benefits with a gastric band and complementary hypnotic scripts. Consider this book as an outline of natural remedies for your lifetime recovery from unpleasant body and weight-related issues. Always track the changes in your weight, emotions and another daily life routine between each script that you listen to every 3-4 days a week. Then compare these notes for your awareness about how your body and mind respond to them. This book demonstrates training and qualification for providing direction to those who are not well equipped for solving a problem related to the daily life eating process. This is a short and time-saving opportunity to feel fit and smart yet beautiful internally and externally with the minimum investment ever made.

The following will be used throughout the scripts for ease during the art of narration.

Long pause=10-20 seconds (indicated with L.P and will be given x2 or x3 if used more than once/number of times to be used will be specified)

Middle Pause=5-8 seconds (M.P, other instructions are same as above for frequency)

Short pause=2-3 seconds (S.P, other instructions are same as above for frequency)

1. Meditation for preparation

Let's get ready for a wonderful experience

This experience takes you towards relaxation

The relaxation that you would like to have in your daily routine

You are here, listening to these preparation steps

(S.P after each of the above statements)

You are willing completely to turn your life into success many times more than you already have

You may be doing this for the first time or maybe not

You still tend to feel it a new and rich experience loaded with ease and satisfaction as its outcome

Be favourable to yourself and get started to generously progress into the world, which is full of creative methods to heal

(M.P after each of the above statements)

You are ready now

(L.P)

Whatever you are going through in routine

That is all just a temporary effect of what influence comes to you

You are beyond those worries, hardships, negativity and disappointments

You are taking the hold of converting your losses into profits

The time you have chosen to prepare your body and mind to relax is feasible

You are about to appropriately focus on the existence of yours in this universe

You are going to beautifully touch the possibilities of achieving your dreams

You have the potential to connect with the power of your mind

You can allow creativity to shape your destiny

(M.P after each of the above statements)

Find a comfortable place where you can sit straight or lie down preferably

Make sure your arms and feet are relaxed

It must be easy enough for you to feel the weight of your body on the furniture

You are now grounded with nature

You will transfer the despairs onto the unseen particles of the universe and become light, pure and valuable

Make sure there is no voice around you but you can listen to your heartbeats

Slowly try to close your eyes and dig deep into the world of transformation

(S.PX3 after each of the above statements)

You are going to meditate through all your sensory perceptions

(L.PX2)

Breathing is what you do all the time

Today is the time and opportunity for you to deeply explore and be grateful for what you are capable to do better and notice how it flows

The flow of the breathing making your diaphragm expands and shrinks in a rhythmic manner

You are attentive towards the motion of the natural process with so much power that you rarely recognize before

Today realize how you breathe deeply

Inhale deeply and notice the effect for three seconds, 1, 2, and 3

Hold on and notice the self-control for three seconds, 1, 2, and 3

Exhale and release air for three seconds, 1, 2, and 3

Well done!

(M.PX2 after each of the above statements)

Imagine, there are green grasslands in front of you

You are sitting in the middle of the greens for a long time

You can feel the coldness of the earth and the warmness of the air

The soil is friendly for you and your body temperature is comfortable for exploration of this place

Without any distraction, you are with your eyes closed sitting in a peaceful environment

Notice that your surroundings are safe

You continue to focus on breathing and how the breathing rhythms are mesmerizing your soul

(L.P after each of the above statements)

In the depths of your soul, there is a place like the one you imagine in your surroundings

Get down in the depths of your soul

Imagine there is a staircase leading you to the room of your soul that cooperates with your mind and body *(M.P after each of the above statements)*

With me imagine the movement of your feet from 1-10 on the stairs going down keeping your attention in the middle of your body, 1, 2, 3, 4, 5, 6, 7, 8, 9, 10 (S.P between each)

Now you are at the depth of your soul and the natural green, peaceful place is in front of you

Fresh air is blowing and you continue to breathe deeply

Relaxation is spreading all over your body from the centre of your soul

Your attention is on the centre of your soul where you can feel the relaxation is spreading all over your body

With the progress of each moment, each muscle within your body is getting more and more relaxed

The relaxation is in your muscles spreading from the core of your body to the extremities

(L.P after each of the above statements)

Your stomach is relaxed, your arms are relaxed, and your hands, palms, fingers, nails, chest, neck and face are all relaxed (M.P between each body part)

Relaxation is in your hips, lower back, thighs, legs, feet, heels, soles and toes (M.P between each body part)

Let the thoughts come and go

There is no way to stop them

They are like fresh air and they have no power within themselves

The power is in your attention

Pay attention to your relaxation

You can deep breath and stay relaxed in any situation when the power of your mind focuses on the positivity and happiness, success and achievement, your goals and goals directed action

Mind have thoughts, beliefs and they are rarely factual

Let you free of their influence and deep breathe once again

(M.PX2 after each of the above statements)

Next to your thoughts, you feel emotions

Emotions that are natural, intense and short-lived

You might know your emotions when you react based on them

You are allowed to feel joy, happiness, satisfaction and ease as much as you want

Focus on the moments most of the time in which you laugh openly

Find ways to put a smile on the faces of other people as much as you can

Believe this that you can accept all the love, passion and energy to feel happy

Draw all the positive emotions you have been noticing since childhood

(L.P after each of the above statements)

Let all your actions aligned with your positive emotions

Let all your love direct you to compassion, love and kindness filled acts

Let this introspection of your own experiences flow with the forces that you experience from your surroundings

Notice the enthusiasm and complete familiarity of the internal and external world

The soul and mind works about the body, manifested in actions and behaviours we do all day and night

This appears to establish a connection for better outcomes and productivity

Your productivity determines your success and you are moving ahead to achieve all that you want to achieve

(S.PX2 after each of the above statements)

You must learn the art of managing triggers for moving ahead smoothly

Overcome the challenges by identifying the triggers that stop you from success

The triggers can be managed

They can be a place, a time, an object, a person or an activity that possibly hinders the state of relaxation in your life

You can witness the most relaxed environment daily

Relaxation in the visual scenes in front of your eyes

Relaxation in the voices you hear and the sounds you hear

Relaxation may come with all the textures you touch and the smell you smell and the taste you taste

(S.P after each of the above statements)

Settle yourself to gain control over you completely

Self-control comes with ease as you start to believe that you can control yourself

You may feel the self-control and the power of gaining control all over your mind and body

In all the states of your mental capacity whether it be joy, peace and contentment

Self-control is present there

It progresses and manages to be a part of your actions regularly

You are about to open your existence for a magical and powerful creation of the universe

Let's absorb the deep blessings of health

(M.P after each of the above statements)

Feel the light that is entering every cell of your body to make you comfortable and fully prepared to attain the chain of behaviours that encourages you and stimulates you to progress the relaxation

All the light, a very bright shimmer is now prevailing throughout the body from head to toe and flowing like the thin sheet of water

The light has a soothing effect on your head, the skin of your forehead, feel this light on your cheeks and chin

Feel the light on your neck and shoulders; the light now covers your arms and abdomen

The light now covers your lower body parts

(L.P after each of the above statements)

There is a purpose of the light to spread upon you

It is meant to spread the good virtues, wisdom, patience and morality

It has all that you ever want to seek from the depths of your soul

You are obtaining more and more bravery

You are attaining more and more wisdom

You are more driven to pick the healthy foods

Today is the first day of your journey to pick the food for relaxation

You most of the time eat only for relaxation and you choose to eat only when you are relaxed

(S.P after each of the above statements)

Imagine your real life

The hours in which you feel most pleasure and most fulfilled sense of existence

In real life, you decide to focus on mindfulness all the time

Whatever you do you do it mindfully

You sit, stand, walk, eat, talk, meet and greet people mindfully

You recall the minute details of every hour you spend alive

You do breathing and deep breathing that goes on deeper and deeper for your blood flow to feel

You are indeed at the deepest levels of your peace

Your hair is peace and your perception is peace, your outer is peace and your inner is peace

(S.P after each of the above statements)

Peace is similar to the greenery on which you began imagining the progressive relaxation for your peace

Scan the muscles again for your awareness about how you have built the capacity to relocate peace whenever and wherever you want

You scan your head, face, body and feet; there is a flow of peace and happiness that you have seen

At this point, you are once again witnessing the beauty of nature, the smell of soil, the warm and cold temperatures of the air and grass around you

Your body weight has become lighter like a feather and you are ready to fly with the power of your mind

(S.P after each of the above statements)

Coming back to the surface from the depths of your soul is about to happen

When you come back you may apply the peaceful actions as your habit

In all the situations in which you ever live

You can face the challenges with calmness

You are prepared for a bigger achievement and success for the sake of your own life

You potentially get the happiest outcome from this experience as you come along with my voice

Imagine there is a door in the depths of your soul

The place where you are right now

(S.P after each of the above statements)

The same staircase is going upward in the form of 10 stairs (S.P)

You may climb up towards the external world, one at a time, slowly and with peace 1, 2, 3, 4, 5, 6, 7, 8, 9, and 10 (S.P between each number)

Deep breathe as you are out of that staircase in the place of meditation

You have reached the place from where we moved ahead to the glorious success of achieving your ideal body

Open your eyes to the physical objects that are present around you

(M.P after each of the above statements)

You are feeling the heights of your physical and mental competency

With a new perspective to the situations, you daily visit

With a new ambition to meet the people you already know and those who you don't

Your confidence is limitless and there are no boundaries to the exposure

(M.P after each of the above statements)

Praise once your creativity and imagination

Your drive to attract the tolerance and patience

Your self-control is at the peak of your mind

(S.P after each of the above statements)

Your best supply to overcome the barriers to your irrational beliefs is the self-control you have managed to possess (L.P)

Be grateful with open hands, spread arms and say thank you universe!

2. Flexibility in beliefs

Try to sit completely relaxed, as you feel deeply and deeply relaxed you feel that there is no distraction around you

The only voice that you hear in your ears is mine

You need to listen to my voice very carefully

And when you do this, you feel if there are any voices from your environment, they fade away

Here you must assure yourself that through following my voice carefully you will not only benefit from weight loss but also your beliefs will be flexible while you intend to choose a food to eat

Get ready for the helpful suggestions and close your eyes smoothly

(S.P after each of the above statements)

You might imagine your current situation that you have in your mind about eating healthy and helpful habits

To dig down deeply into your beliefs imagine there is are three slopes that are going down into a basement lounge

Move ahead by choosing one of the slopes that you can imagine and reach to the lounge that is extremely comfortable and relaxing

As you pick one of the slopes, move ahead and by moving forward you may face a large lounge

In this lounge, sit on a sofa with your favourite cloth lining

(L.PX2 after each of the above statements)

Again choose one of your best feelings that you would like to gain through this programming of your mind

To become leaner, smarter, healthier and slimmer

Take a long and deep breath and continue doing it

The best feeling that you choose to focus on today throughout this journey of flexibility in beliefs could be energetic, alert and solid

The feeling that you pick here must be a presenter of your outcome

The outcome that you seek after losing heavy amounts of fat

As you lose more and more fat from your body the weight sheds off

(M.P after each of the above statements)

Pay attention to your deep nice breaths

Let this fat off not only from your body but the mind and your whole life permanently

You can facilitate this process with the help of your beliefs

When you believe you are becoming slimmer because you are losing fat with hypnosis

You would see it coming, now take it easy and comfortable

You are the only person who can make it happen with your willpower and the power of your mind

Into this deep comfortable lounge, you have chosen a feeling that is completely aligned with your belief about yourself following the weight loss

(S.P after each of the above statements)

Imagine a setting where you would like to become flexible

More and more flexible not only physically and psychologically

When your body is flexible you can move freely but when your mind is flexible you can cope with any challenge that comes in your way and interfere with the achievement of goals

Your health goals are as important as your mind

So let your mind be more open, flexible and enjoy the sense of being liberal

Imagine a scene where you would like this change to happen

(S.PX3 after each of the above statements)

Believe it that within the next few minutes, you will recondition your total existence of mind and beliefs

You will turn yourself in a leaner and smarter you

Your eating habits will improve and with your new self-image you will groom your body

Enjoy these moments of change

Imagine your mind is a rubber band and it is stretching and stretching to a point where it allows you to insert some very interesting views that you didn't know

For example, you live not only healthy but happy as well with your new eating routine

(M.PX2 after each of the above statements)

This place is your mind, all between the stretch of this rubber band that you imagine you are allowed to rethink some of the very unhelpful beliefs that you ever have about your eating behaviours and can turn them into helpful ones

You will able to enjoy your life in future and feel satisfied with your eating habits as much as you were before

Now, pick one of the beliefs that you would like to change

For this transformation remember to add this belief into the middle of the stretched rubber band

(S.P after each of the above statements)

Observe own thoughts, how did they appear in the first place

Maybe the beliefs come from childhood experiences

Maybe the beliefs are strengthened by social pressure

Maybe role models teach the beliefs

Maybe the beliefs are the results of experimentation in your teenage

There may be hundreds of reasons and possible combination and interaction of factors behind it

You are still free to flexible your beliefs

Focus on imagining an alternative to the belief you have picked to transform today

In the middle of the rubber band, your belief becomes flexible

(S.P after each of the above statements)

Identify the various effects of the irrational belief that you have chosen to insert into a rubber band

It might have changed the way you look at your body

It might have influenced your eating habits

It might have modified your view about your life

Now imagine stretching that rubber band a bit more

As you stretch the rubber band you feel that the band is getting more and more glossy and beautiful

As the band gets more beautiful you feel that your belief towards unhelpful eating is reforming into a helpful one

(S.P after each of the above statements)

Challenge the unhelpful belief at this point now focus again

As you stretch the rubber band you feel that the band is getting more and more glossy and beautiful

As the band gets more beautiful you feel that your belief towards unhelpful eating is reforming into a helpful

If you have believed that eating more than needed to keep you away from food for longer hours

Challenge this unhelpful and irrational belief with this affirmation

Eating only when hungry and only healthy keeps my stomach filled and satisfied for 4-6 hours

(S.P after each of the above statements)

Finding alternatives is an amazing way to create flexible beliefs

There is always more than one way to think about a situation

The need for food is physiological

There is no relation of food requirement with the time to eat

It varies for everyone in different situations

There is a much more helpful way to eat as intended by nature

Eating the amount of food equals to our fist and so on

The extra storage of fat is the result of eating more than required by the body

So, here one of the beliefs is flexible for your help in transforming the body from fat-containing to healthy

(S.P after each of the above statements)

Now you have experienced how to think in dialects

Thinking in a dialectical manner means thinking in two different dimensions for your ease

You might consider a belief negatively and then needs to rethink to make it positive

Whenever you feel the need to imagine an alternative and flexible belief

Imagine a rubber band stretched to an extent that you could put it in an old belief to generate options

In this way, your flexibility in beliefs grow even more and more

(S.P after each of the above statements)

Affirm your capacity to lose weight and fat by eating less and less than you burn

Eat fewer calories than you burn

Eat less fat than you loose

Day by day try to follow this rule

Eating into the limits of body requirements would also enable you to think in different dialects

Adjusting the meal according to fewer calories and measuring food for less fat and more proteins or less simple carbohydrates and more complex carbohydrates excite your mind for more alternatives to prepare and consume the food

(S.P after each of the above statements)

Becoming open-mindedness is like a rubber band stretched at ease without any force or difficulty

Your mind is also a rubber band and it works like one at least to reprogram into a new you

A new you are a healthy eater, a healthy cook and a healthy person with complete satisfaction

To reduce weight, gather some flexible beliefs about how to meet your body requirements without much food

And repeat this pattern until you achieve your ideal weight and figure

The inert fat needs to be released and the daily food must not exceed what you released

As you take part in this initiative you will feel much more potential in you

(S.P after each of the above statements)

Focus again on your own beliefs about food and weight and your body image

Learn to be mindful of your beliefs daily few minutes

Spend few minutes before you try to eat something

What do you think of the food you eat?

Observe all the experiences that elicit your mind related to your eating habits

It can be related to the quantity of food or quality of food or the outcome of the food you intend you eat

(S.P after each of the above statements)

Settle your thoughts that come to your mind into the rubber band and rethink to reprogram the thoughts

This is one of the easiest ways to seek flexibility in your beliefs and allowing yourself to think in different aspects

As an outcome, you observe each day that how you make a difference in your eating habits and overall self-image

As compared to your past your some of the beliefs have now rescreened for a better future

You are a quick learner and I have complete trust in your competency to achieve an ideal weight

(S.P after each of the above statements)

Remember, no matter what procedure would you use for measuring the food you eat in terms of calories and fat

A weight scale is also a flexible tool

Note that you are going to continue a flexible journey

The measurement varies for everyone and depending on your activity and circumstances plus the food quality

Find a variety of options for your measured diet and support a good storage system for the leftovers

Whatever you do the only thing you need to focus on is flexibility both mentally and physically

So now do more brainstorming, create new cells, move your body freely and survive at your best

(S.P after each of the above statements)

Coming back from the world of flexibility

Be grateful for few seconds towards your capacity to reach here

You have decided to allow more flexibility in your beliefs and storing more food in the fridge than in your body

At your convenience, you are doing good at a great deal

Cut off the past and start a new day for a better tomorrow with the patterns of healthy eating

(S.P after each of the above statements)

As you have understood the easy and quick method to seek flexibility in beliefs

Again take a sweet and slow breath

Feel rested and deeply rested as much as you can

You are getting lighter and lighter like air in the balloon with readiness to turn your beliefs about food from irrational to rational

You seem prepared to get action on your food eating patterns

(S.P after each of the above statements)

You might imagine the same lounge you started in

In this lounge, you are on a sofa with your favourite cloth lining

Take a look at the lounge and find the slopes to go back upwards from the depths and dungeons of your mind where all your beliefs are deeply rooted

Imagine there is are three slopes that are going upward back into your place where you began listening to my voice

Move ahead by choosing one of the slopes that you can imagine and reach safely

As you pick one of the slopes, move ahead and by moving forward you may feel relieved and lighter

Open your eyes and you are ready to take action on your healthy life

(L.PX2 after each of the above statements)

3. Placing the gastric band

Settle yourself to a place where you feel most comfortable

This is the continuation of a wonderful journey towards success

This is your success and you can attain the completion of your desires

The desires that you have been asking for fulfilment is now very close to your presence

You are about to achieve a desirable body weight to your satisfaction

You are going to satisfy yourself with the best ideal body image that you always wanted to have

You are mentally prepared to receive the gift of the universe that you have been yearning for a lot for months

(M.P after each of the above statements)

Make sure you are present on soft bedding or sofa in a room full of quietness

Let the position of your body completely loose and stay straight to feel all the weight of your body completely resting on the furniture

As you feel relaxed and your body gets heavy, your eyes are becoming heavy

Continue feeling the heaviness on your eyelids

Now close your eyes softly and tighten the closed eyes

The eyes are getting tighter and tighter as you close them

You are going to experience a warm change in your beautiful body

(S.P after each of the above statements)

Imagine you are on the first step of your success ladder

This step is warm and welcoming for you

To change what you want to change in your body feel the warmness to the depths of your core

The middle of your body is the powerhouse for transformation

Get more and more relaxed as you breathe rhythmically (Repeat twice)

(S.P after each of the above statements)

Let you breathe deeper and deeper as you imagine the sea breeze coming towards your face and touch your skin politely

There is a peace that flows everywhere in a pattern spreading all over your body in a form of a network

Notice that pattern for relaxation

That is providing relaxation in your head, ears, face, eyes, neck, shoulders, arms, hands, palms, fingers, chest, stomach, thighs, lower back, legs, feet, toes and heels (S.P after each body part)

You are feeling relaxed in each of your body parts and muscles are getting looser and looser that allows you to feel completely free for a change

Your body might lay straight with an erect spine

As you observe the natural curve of your backbone at the back of your body weight

You notice how the relaxation is flowing in a rhythmic pattern all over your body as naturally as possible

(L.P after each of the above statements)

Try to inhale as much deeper as possible

Through your nose, you inhale for three seconds

Then you hold the breathing for three seconds

Then you exhale for three seconds and blow the air out gradually and completely

Continue this process and you may feel how the lungs get full with fresh air as you inhale and the stomach spreads out as well

Upon exhale, your stomach shrinks and lungs flatten as the air goes out of your mouth in a flow

Through this process, the body parts feel the relief from tension to relaxation, from tightness to calmness and looseness

(S.P after each of the above statements)

Bundles of oxygen arrive in each cell of your body with inhaling

And the carbon dioxide, impure air and toxins leave out from your body through exhaling

You are completely aware of the feeling when the stomach shrinks and moves towards the back of your body near the backbone

The flesh of your stomach appears flat and as you imagine it gets flat and flat as much as you need

You are full of energy and positivity with the hope and ease of feeling a flat stomach throughout your life

(M.P after each of the above statements)

Today is the day to realize the ideal image is very close to you and as you desire more about it imagine more about it

It will get closer and you feel that your stomach flatness is in your control

As you want to feel your stomach the extra fat is shedding off your stomach area

You have taken the responsibility to burn the fat off your body from all over the body parts that are loaded with the excessive body fat

Affirm this change for your body that you love the most "I am bringing the change in my body for a flat physique and fat burning attitude" (Repeat)

(L.P after each of the above statements)

Remind yourself that "I do for my body what I want and I feel love and kindness towards my body, I accept my body as it is flattening and reaching to the desired shape and desired weight".

Affirm as you are in the deepest relaxation

Imagine yourself in a state around a soothing breeze

You are in a camp with mountains full of green grass all over the way you look

The camp has deep light and flame contains a scent of rose

The tent of the camp is a shimmer as if stars are all above your skin

(S.P after each of the above statements)

Absorbing this mesmerizing scent, the mountains are sprinkling snow

The snow seems to glow like a purple tint of the sky

The tip of the sky looks glorious and secure

In this wonderful cosy mood of the surroundings

You spread your arms to invite the ideal image of yours

Keep looking at this site and clench your fist once very tight

As quickly as possible now release the tightness and let your fears go away

All of your muscles are relaxed and loose

The body is deeply loose and heavy at the centre of the stomach

(L.P after each of the above statements)

As you try to go down deeper in your body walk down towards the centre in ten steps with my voice

1

2

3

4

5

5

6

7

8

9

10

You are on the deepest end of the centre of your body

Move few steps and take a complete view of your destination

This is where you want a change, a transformation and this is where you need to relax

As you are willing to change your body delightfully

Seek the help of this universe and let the power functions for your desire fulfilment

Let the senses perceive the stomach at the deepest level

(S.P after each of the above statements)

You agree with your body to freely let go of the emotional and physical burden harmlessly

The load you have been carrying is swishing away as you embrace a gastric band around your stomach with an open heart

Accept the gastric band on this place of your stomach where most of the weight, burden and fat lives

A gastric band is placed along your waistline

This is the same part where your physical, mental and emotional exhaustion are placed as well that you have been experiencing so far

This gastric band influences your fat burning, accelerates the vanishing of undesirable pounds and reduce your tendency to gain undesirable weight on your stomach

(M.P after each of the above statements)

Be aware of your body there is a gastric band on your stomach

You have accepted that gastric band and you adjust to it

You are mindful and ready to maximize the happiness that this gastric band placement is offering you

Imagine the gastric band on your stomach visually; listen to your breathing with a gastric band placed on your stomach

Feel the gastric band is glowing and soft

You are in love with this tiny band around your stomach

(M.PX2 after each of the above statements)

And as you meet the gastric band closely you may feel the optimal sense of health, courage and energy

As you observe the gastric band, your curiosity extends

A vivid sketch of the gastric band is a thin and small belt

Let me discuss with you that the gastric band is placed around your stomach in your favourite colour

This band is perfect somewhat larger than the size of your fist

The gastric band's colour gives you joy and the texture of the gastric band is flashing as if you are seeing an entertaining screen

The gastric band is of your choice

You choose the gastric band that is best for you

(S.P after each of the above statements)

The placement of the gastric band is a success for you

Your first success in the best shape that you love

Notice the gastric band is placed exactly on the position where it is needed to restrict the amount of food you eat daily

Your daily food consumption is getting smaller and smaller in portion but more and more delicious and nutritious

As the process of eating slows down for you

You recognize the fullness, lightness and usefulness of the food that you eat throughout the day only when you are hungry

(S.PX2 after each of the above statements)

The gastric band placed around your stomach on the area where fat is in excess

The gastric band is making your stomach smaller and flatter

This gastric band is the solution to treat your body weight without any medical procedure

The gastric band is creative that motivates you to manage your weight effortlessly

All around your stomach your gastric band is helping in the quick digestion of your food

You get the nutrients from your daily food

Concentrate on the skin of your stomach

The skin is getting tighter and tighter to support the internal organs as the fat burns out and release from the stomach area

(S.PX3 after each of the above statements)

Imagine the fat-releasing out of all other areas of your body

As you feel fat burns the body feels lighter and there is little hunger that you feel afterwards

Each time you eat, you eat only a small portion of healthy and natural food

The sources of food that you buy usually is free of fats, sodium and simple sugar

Anytime you can eat your favourite food

Continue focusing on the gastric band placed on your stomach

Whenever you feel hungry and eat something you enjoy with the presence of the gastric band

Identify the signs of hunger in your body that signals you to eat

(S.PX4 after each of the above statements)

There are signs that signals to stop eating when you eat

Listen to the full stomach feeling

The gastric band minimizes your eating because now you eat only the adequate amount of food that your body needs

You are ready to live a healthy life

This gives you a feeling of satisfaction, fulfilment and happiness

Your mind is relaxed, your body is calm and your stomach flattens as you closely observe the gastric band placement for your good

Once again appreciate the benefits of the gastric band that is placed on your stomach

(S.P after each of the above statements)

Take a deep breath and recall the presence of your concentration on the core of your stomach area with the most body fat

This accumulation is now getting out from the depths of your stomach

This amazes you as if you are on a vacation

There is a camp in which you are resting

Noticing the sky and allowing the tiny snowdrops letting you feel cold and calm

The gastric band supply you with deeper observation skills, awareness and mindful appreciation of the slightest changes under the skin of your stomach

Your total body weight lessens and gives you admiration for choosing it as your lifestyle

(S.P after each of the above statements)

Wherever you go this gastric band stays with you

You can sit, stand, sleep, eat and do all the routine tasks with this gastric band

This band is like a piece of cloth on your skin

As you move it stays with you

You are comfortable with this gastric band

It gives you an ideal body image and your desirable feelings of beauty

The gastric band is a part of your body

You are thankful for this choice of yours

You make decisions for yourself and the decisions are good for your health

(S.P after each of the above statements)

Come back from the depths of your core

Your body is reached to a state of fitness without any undesirable effect

Come up to the surroundings where you comfortably lay down on a smooth surface

As you hear my voice counting 10-1 imagine yourself getting out of the deepness of your stomach at the core of your body

10

9

8

7

6

5

4

3

2

1

Here you are in your new world where you can see the most soothing objects of nature

There is a natural smell of the air around you

You can feel the taste of your pleasure

Listen to any sound that you can hear

Move ahead to a fresh start.

(S.P after each of the above statements)

4. Affirmations for self-satisfaction

Let's get relaxed

It is a blessing to sit relaxed

Every day we strive to get better and better

Just like that strive to get more and more deeply relaxed

This is the time to leave your hands and palms completely open and allow yourself to receive the most useful and blessed sense of self-satisfaction within you

Self-satisfaction is grown daily and makes you the best version of yourself

As you know that in this world we all try to become the best version of ourselves to achieve the best

With full of adventurous experiences and incredible knowledge you can grab the satisfaction you seek

(S.P after each of the above statements)

In whatever position you are

Become the most relaxed person on earth

Loosen your limbs

Loosen your body

Make sure you are wearing loose and soft clothes

Your bedding is soft and you are breathing in and out with the deepest inhale and exhale movements

Nice

Focus on relaxation once again and scan all your body parts one by one from head to toe if there are any tensions simply contract those muscles and count for three seconds

Now release and smile nicely, openly and deeply

(S.P after each of the above statements)

Pay attention to your eyes

Make sure the light is dim in your room

Make sure there is no distraction around you

Your eyes are getting heavier and heavier as you continue breathing

Breathing with heavy eyes is making your eyes even heavier

Don't try to blink your eyes

Avoid blinking and let it imagine that you are sleeping to deeply feel the feelings of satisfaction

As few movements pass you feel that the eyes are about to close

Now as it feels difficult to keep the eyes open

Close them tightly and make you relaxed

(S.P after each of the above statements)

Imagine the eating patterns that you usually observe in yourself

These patterns might mostly let you eat more than your body needs

Excessive eating makes your food store extra calories more easily

The carbohydrates when in excess they are also stored in your body in the form of fats

Similarly, the fat is stored in the form of fats and your body becomes bigger and bigger than the ideal one

To combat this outcome we seek satisfaction

We need to readily feel satisfied with the amount of the food we eat

(S.P after each of the above statements)

You may have an idea that the amount of food you used to eat in the past didn't satisfy you earlier

Even there might be some times when the food you consumed didn't satisfy you at all

Lack of knowledge about food consumption may become a barrier between you and your weight loss

But you are now ready to turn your dissatisfaction into satisfaction

Whatever you do and feel and eat is totally in your hands

Your wisdom tells you that you can feel totally satisfied when you begin eating healthy and emerged yourself as a completely new person

(S.P after each of the above statements)

Imagine now to satisfy yourself, your hunger, your stomach and your body needs with the help of eating less and burning more calories and fats

You continue losing fat and excessive calories by eating lesser and lesser

This becomes a regular compulsion for you to eat lesser and burn more fat calories

In this way, your fat stores are ended and you will come out as a slimmer, leaner and healthier you

Replace the old patterns of eating more and burning fewer calories and fat off your skin with eating less and burning more and more calories and fats

Imagine your extra weight pounds are now melting and melting and melting with great intensity

With the eyes of your mind, you are capable to see yourself satisfied deeply with the image of yourself that is now relaxed, calm, healthy and slim

There is plenty of food but you feel satisfied

There are plenty of choices but you intend to pick only those with the lowest calories possible

You enjoy drinking water at ease

You love colourful fruits and vegetables in small portions

Because you are satisfied with them deeply

(S.P after each of the above statements)

Planning and setting goals for your healthy life in advance is one of the most beneficial tricks to keep your mouth open for healthy foods only and only at the time of need

Chew the freshest and raw foods with lots of vitamins and minerals and that is all you need most of the time

Then along with it, you have a choice to pick lightly cooked, boiled or grilled lean meat and olives to accompany the whole-wheat bun

Add some greens, seeds and nuts to make it even more exotic and you are satisfied with one of your daily meals

(S.P after each of the above statements)

Taking actions upon your goals is not to shame but to feel pride

This proud you do in your decision making is the satisfaction

There is satisfaction in every sip of your water if you explore

There is satisfaction in each bite of the food you must consume if you wish to observe

Making a daily habit to write the food observations and eating experiences in a journal by the end of the day is an excellent to practice self-satisfaction

(S.P after each of the above statements)

Evaluating alternatives is another step to achieve satisfaction with your food

This is an honour to take part in your food practices

Leave the worries and avail the accessible choices to pick and pack for your bag

Participate in the storage of your healthy food in the forms of bites; fingers and crisps within zip-lock plastic bags

These tiny bags are good to invest within for your most valuable life

Even if you put the smallest bite in your bag from your leftover veggies and corn burrito or a cutlet you will be able to burn little calories and at least avoiding the addition of many more calories that are not required between the meals and before the eating timings by not buying anything unhealthy from the market when you are away from home and your regular food storage

With tiny portions of healthy food, you would be able to manage your odd cravings and appetite

When these cravings and appetite are satisfied your body stays safe permanently from the damage you intend you make with a packaged food

Few choices can save you from impulsive acts of binge eating and addictive artificial flavours

(S.P after each of the above statements)

Affirmations to bring a positive shift in body and mind must always be filled in your routine

Read them, write them, recall them, memorize them, remind them or verbalize them, paste them around you in written form with a suitable motivating image or draw yourself, keep them in your file, pocket or drawer they have the sensitive power to self-hypnotize you and satisfy at the deepest level

Some of them are "I have willingness and determination to manage my cravings and controlling my binge eating episodes, sizes are only numbers they don't define me, I believe that matters"

(S.P after each of the above statements)

Keep moving and repeat it with me with more focus and attention, slowly and with understanding

Register each of these words one by one

"I have willingness and determination to manage my cravings and controlling my binge eating episodes, sizes are only numbers they don't define me, I believe that matters"

Register each of these words one by one

"I have willingness and determination to manage my cravings and controlling my binge eating episodes, sizes are only numbers they don't define me, I believe that matters" (Now repeat each word with S.P)

You do it great now for the one last time say

"I have willingness and determination to manage my cravings and controlling my binge eating episodes, sizes are only numbers they don't define me, I believe that matters"

This was one of the astonishing dares that you just passed brilliantly and beautifully

The courage and the bravery that you have is mostly the care you show to yourself

As you feel more and more satisfied with your body and self-image the self-satisfaction flows in and out of your heart enlightening you and those around you glamorously

(S.P after each of the above statements)

Achievement of dreams is possible if you care about your peace go for your dreams

Visualize your dream of achieving satisfaction daily

Observe and describe the characteristics of your ideal satisfaction

Note the related emotions, beliefs, words, symbols and let yourself love the art of giving and receiving with this exchange of dreams with reality

This idea is fantastic and so does you

(S.P after each of the above statements)

Success in satisfaction is any act of kindness that you show towards yourself and others

It can be selecting a clever food or tantalizing natural herb for your meal

It can be a lovely, outstanding and wonderful dish that you cook for a friend

Or it can be an extra bag of chips or any other unhealthy food that you donate to someone in need

All of this shows you satisfaction to give something and in return, you may receive bundles of satisfaction

Forget the past mistakes they matter no more

There is nothing more beautiful than the path of success to achieve a thread to hold and follow your dreams

(S.P after each of the above statements)

With the solid belief in your food-making skills and ability to use natural food for health creatively

Make a pout to fly a soft kiss away from your mouth in the universe as a token of thanks for guiding you to success and satisfaction

Be restful and peaceful to every bit of your body, each inch of your skin and the minute cells, your organs and the blood flowing within

(S.P after each of the above statements)

Settle your mind to take in the above-given suggestions deeply to root in your mind

Your mind sees the images of the optimal satisfaction that you seek in your daily life for your body and eating habits

Whatever you do you feel satisfied and succeeded, there is plenty of hope and positivity in your beliefs as you affirm the self-satisfaction and understand the mechanism of feeling satisfied the level of your satisfaction exceeds moment by moment without any hurdles

It doesn't matter how you temporarily feel but the satisfaction matters with the long-term effect and influence on your mind and soul

(S.P after each of the above statements)

Now again focus on the relaxation that has reached the depths of your body

Feel that you are the most relaxed person on earth

Your limbs are loose and your body is loose, weightless and carefree

You breathe in and out with the deepest inhale and exhale movements

Nice

Focus on relaxation one last time and scan all your body parts one by one from head to toe if there are any tensions simply contract those muscles and count for three seconds

Now release and smile nicely, openly and deeply

(S.P after each of the above statements)

You may open your eyes now and manifest the visualization with your perception

As you are satisfied you feel much more love and tenderness for your body and you treat it with a recovered self-satisfaction, the past leaves off the corner of your mind

You are worthy enough to put effort and time into the planning of food that you eat

You attend to your body weight and shape and you stop running from it but you own it as it is and feel its beauty with the most compassionate eyes that have unconditional love and empty judgments

(S.P after each of the above statements)

5. Embrace your emotions

Find an area in your home with dim lights

Choose a place with the least noises around you

Choose a place without any visual distractions

Get yourself ready for a pleasurable experience containing a lot of sensory outcomes

Become relaxed in a situation where you get easily engaged in the process of visualizing and manifesting your ideal emotional stability

Take a look at some point in front of you

Maybe a wall where you can focus for a long time

Try to open your eyes without blinking as much as you can

Let your eyes close gently when you feel they are tired

Take your time

(L.PX2 after each of the above statements)

As you feel your eyes are closed and you can experience the feelings that are associated with your current emotional status

Whatever your feelings are let them go

Release the clutter of your mind that have been upsetting you for a long time

Try to feel most comfortable and recall an event from your life that previously and effortlessly caused you laughter

Remember that laughter

Imagine your voices of laughing and your facial expressions

Notice the textures you felt that time and the movements of your overall posture

(L.PX2 after each of the above statements)

Suppose that your desire to become slim and slender is a realistic wish

Still, look at your emotions that are associated with this desire

I count till seven and you would notice some of the emotions that elicited by the idea of this desire

1

2

3

4

5

6

7

To be honest, most of the emotions and feelings attached to this desire may be negative

As they can be shame, guilt, disappointment and hopelessness

This is natural due to the failures in the past to achieve this desire

(L.P after each of the above statements)

Take a nice deep breath for three seconds

1

2

3

And realize, on the other hand, the emotions associated with the desire to become slim and slender might be positive for example, hope, success, happiness, satisfaction

Now try to feel more and more deeply and deeply calm

This is just the start of your recognition for this emotional stability possibility that you might have resisted so far

Achieving emotional stability and peace is a skill to learn, master and practice

Continue focusing on your breathing once again

(S.P after each of the above statements)

Your emotions are the triggers for your actions

Emotions are also very intense but short-lived

But the impact they would have on your mental health is long-term

Feel the intensity of the emotions that you feel when you look at the food

Feel the intensity of the emotions that you feel when you avoid certain foods

Feel the intensity of the emotions that you feel when you look at your body weight

Feel the intensity of the emotions that you feel when you feel something about your physique

(S.P after each of the above statements)

Depth of all the emotions that you have just tried to look at is the real feelings that may be good or bad

All kinds of such feelings are very much strong and the potential of these emotions can make your stability stick to your healthy diet or can break your integrity with your outlook towards food

The emotions that you have just identified can be a motivator or a breaker of your healthy food routine

Yes, this is for your awareness to manage your emotions wisely for the best weight loss outcomes

(S.P after each of the above statements)

What you think of yourself also elicits an emotion

Imagine the feeling when you look at yourself in the mirror

Imagine the feeling when you look at your food plate on the dining table

Imagine the feeling when you look at your wardrobe and pick a dress to wear

Imagine the feeling when you look at yourself in a picture from a party

All these emotions that are related to different events are actually what lead you to a healthy routine following or unhealthy routine following

(S.P after each of the above statements)

Are there myths that are attached to your emotions and food?

Now observe and get ready to identify and challenge those myths

For example dissatisfaction with the weight reduction

Weight reduction is a moment to cherish and celebrate with the motivation to keep following a healthy routine

Challenge this myth with the following affirmation and correct the falsely held belief

"I am satisfied with my body and weight as it is, I love myself and my healthy routine because it is fruitful for my overall health in the long-term"

Now take a deep nice breath

(S.P after each of the above statements)

You are separate from negative emotions

When you are satisfied with your eating healthy foods behaviour then there is no point in feeling low and disappointed because of it

You need to sort out such contradictions

This is okay to face a contradiction due to separate beliefs and actions but emotions are the glue that connects them very well

Feel that you are becoming more and more slender

It shows that you are happy about it

You are satisfied with the eating behaviours and new foods that you freshly add to your grocery

(S.P after each of the above statements)

Loving-kindness in your heart is a tool to align your emotions and actions in a row following by flexible and positive beliefs

As you chose to eat healthy foods remember that you love your body and you are kind towards your health by doing this

You eat protein for strength and take up most of the water with minerals and vitamins packed food in smaller quantities possible to fit your stomach needs

All of this process is the part of your positive emotions towards yourself

The positive emotions guide you to fill your plate with smaller portions of food

(S.P after each of the above statements)

Colours that spread from your love and kindness towards your body has spread all around your meal

Imagine the colours that you see in lean meats, the rainbow colours that you see in the vegetables, the fruits, the nuts and seeds, the colours that you see in food before peeling and after you peel

You would like to pick some of the foods in your hands and you enjoy how they touch your skin and settle against the softness of your fingers and palms

Open yourself to all the colours in your healthy foods list to set away from the preferences

(S.P after each of the above statements)

Facilitate others in compassion

Play a shared game

Share your food with your loved ones, family members even classmates and anyone who you meet daily

Spread the loving and kindness of your emotional energies outside your body influences

Spreading love and sharing kindness with others often gives you an abundance

The abundance of food, the abundance of health, the abundance of gratitude and the abundance of getting more and more attractive with the emotional stability and self-control

Spread all the good around you and then become ready to get it back in larger quantity from the universe

(S.P after each of the above statements)

Observe that loving and kindness towards yourself and others is making you stronger emotionally

This practice for your emotions benefits you in managing the emotional eating at times

This practice for your emotions stops you from the emotional eating out of boredom or relationship conflicts

This practice for your emotions benefits you in managing the eating unhealthy food or any food in excess

The harmful eating is most of the times the emotional eating

Negative emotions in the background water the actions that hazard your healthy eating practice

(S.P after each of the above statements)

You choose food with a wise mind

You prefer to attain a balance in your diet

The balance in your diet and selection of daily healthy foods is a part of the rational process

The rational process is done by our wise mind that is separated from the emotional mind

When our emotions are managed we can think with a wise mind

Your body tends to choose the foods that give strength and build muscle mass rather than the storage of fats in abundance

Our body craves for fat no more and there will be no additional fat intake and rarely the fat is stored

(S.P after each of the above statements)

You do mindful eating whenever you can identify your emotional triggers and calm them down before choosing foods to eat

Affirm, "I feel strong and free of any heavy fats and starches or sugary foods"

As you affirm feel that there is no appetite for unhealthy foods in your stomach

Imagine and say to yourself that I feel no need to eat sweets

I dislike fat and creams

I have no desire for butter

I don't like ice creams and candies

(S.P after each of the above statements)

Observe and affirm that I eat no excessive food

I eat only when hungry

I take small food bites

I taste and smell the food very well

I see the food and listen to the chew of my food and the bites I take

I eat only a small amount of food

The foods that are unhealthy elicit unpleasant emotions in me and I eat only those foods that give me pleasure

I take my time to enjoy the flavours of the food I consider healthy

I am satisfied with my positive emotions and I focus on skimmed milk and low-fat cheese with low caloric foods

(S.P after each of the above statements)

Continue affirming to yourself that my emotions are not interfering with my food intake

I eat only healthy foods regardless of my emotional experiences

I manage my emotions and allow myself to feel the taste of all the healthy foods completely

I feel much better when I eat in small bites

A small number of foods provide me more value to my goals about a healthy and fit lifestyle

I weigh myself because I am hoping that fat has been shed and weight has been decreased

I want to look attractive and I am making myself attractive more and more as I continue eating better than before

(S.P after each of the above statements)

I only respond to the needs of my body

I am managing my emotions for feeling better and to eat better

Whenever I weigh there is a decrease of a couple of pounds

This happens because I follow a healthy eating and I keep it separate from my emotions

My emotional energies cannot be compensated with my eating habits

I learn to eat easily without the influence of my emotions

I stay mindful always when I eat

(S.P after each of the above statements)

What I get from being a mindful eater is that I can enjoy my life even more with healthy eating

Healthy eating is making my sleep better, my digestion is improved and my overall quality of life is improved

I have improved my skin glow and texture; my skin feels fresh and clear

I feel less clutter in my mind and I manage my stress

I maintain my confidence that boost my motivation

I am doing daily pleasurable activities to keep my energy levels up with less consumption of food and more water intake

I am greatly thankful for this process

(S.P after each of the above statements)

Open your eyes quickly and look at the same point you focused on in the beginning to restore the power of positive emotions you have experienced so far

Tomorrow just

Enjoy a single slice of dark and coarse bread in breakfast

Balance your nutrients by eating a green vegetable in lunch

Blend the dinner with yellow corns and red beans

Mix and experiment with the exotic tasty foods that are available to serve for your health and gathered directly from nature as they mature

(S.P after each of the above statements)

6. Tightening the gastric band

Prepare yourself to get comfortable for a beautiful venture

This venture covers the time in which you can make a lot of change in yourself

Your wish is about to fulfil and a goal is near to achieve

You gracefully and with ease learn the art of staying relaxed and beneficial for your good

Ideal body weight in your mind is manifesting in your real life

You are getting a slim waist and a leaner body, a flat stomach that is coming in your path with satisfying outcomes

Moving forward your satisfaction is the most valuable outcome that is taken into consideration

Slowly, very slowly, you can allow yourself at this moment to peacefully rest against a piece of furniture where you relax deeply

(S.P after each of the above statements)

As you hear my voice, simply straight the back of the body and transfer the weight on the chair or bed wherever you get involved in the transformation without any distraction

Close your eyes as soon as you find yourself calm

As you get your eyes closed tightly feel the heaviness of your body and eyes

Continue paying attention to the surroundings in which you are resting

There is no voice around you, your inner self and outer self there is only calmness

A deep calming sensory perception of yourself at the moment is all in your focus

(S.P after each of the above statements)

Let your mind empty

Vacant your mind from unnecessary ideas

Focus on your sensations of the body

The sensations are all over your body

Let the ideas float off your mind and pay attention to your muscles

Your muscles are absorbing deep relaxation in your head, your ears, your face, your eyes, your neck, shoulders, arms, hands, palms and fingers, your abdomen and your back, your legs and feet and toes and the heels, they are all getting more and more relaxed

As you are deeply relaxed, you are completely focused on the breathing pattern of your lungs

(L.P after each of the above statements)

As you release air from your mouth your body shrinks

As you inhale once again your nose fetches air into the lungs and the chest expands

As I count from one to three, continue paying attention to your breathing pattern

Once, two and three

You feel that breathing is getting deeper and deeper to allow deeper relaxation all around your body

You are motivated enough to stay relaxed and you observe the chest and belly movements

Place one hand of yours on your chest, other on your belly that has the gastric band

(M.P after each of the above statements)

Now confidently breathe as deep as you can and feel it for few seconds

Your hopes are high and your energy is positive

With this power in your mind imagine yourself going down deeper into the depths of your body

At the core where your gastric band is placed

Where the desirable changes are taking place

I repeat the numbers from one to ten and you feel yourself moving deeper into the cells of your body as a direct observer

One

Two

Three

Four

Five

Six

Seven

Eight

Nine

Ten

This is the same place where your gastric band is tied like a belt around your stomach

(S.P after each of the above statements)

At this depth of your core, the vibes are passionate

This shows your willingness to become a successful achiever

Your acceptance is powerful and your attitude towards the gastric band slimness is quite affirmative

One more time affirms, "The change in my body weight is in my control"

Yes believe this that you are attracting the desired body weight, desired body shape and you are getting rid of the unnecessary fat with your muscles

The fat that weighs you down

The fat that has started leaving your body since you put the magical gastric band on your body with excessive belly fat

(M.P after each of the above statements)

This point on your body where the gastric band is placed

You open yourself to bring change

There is no magic but it works like magic

The burden has been released from your belly

Your belly is converted into a slimmer place where the muscles are getting toned

This is happening in the manner you want

Your desire to have smooth change is now getting on a deeper level

Stay true to your commitment to change and continue focusing on the change you desire

The gastric band become tighter than before in the next few minutes

Keep noticing the slightest changes that your body makes

It can be a feeling of lightness after you consume food

You may smell the relaxing scents from the air you breathe

The air around you touches your skin like a weightless feather

The taste of your healthy food choices feels good

Even the sight of your food appears appealing regardless of the choice of food is natural and raw

These sensations are soothing as you feel that clean air is helping with your breathing in symphony like rhythms

There is indeed a whole scenario builds to favour your comfort with the gastric band

(L.P after each of the above statements)

Welcome to the next level of your inner self

Note the voice of your core

The core pleasantly directs you to comes out of your mind and experience the body at its deepest end

At this resting state, shining light is evident for you to imagine the gastric band tied around your stomach

It sticks to your skin and spread like a belt covering all that is undesirable in your life

Your body image is improved, as you stay aware of the gastric band protection from the unpleasant experiences

You might have heard the criticism that is no more a part of your life with the help of the gastric band your positive emotions are maximized

(S.P after each of the above statements)

This is wonderful that your body is secure and the gastric band has been changing your attitude towards the responses from the outer world

You are in charge of your feelings, you choose only and you choose only the pleasurable ones

Imagine the cheerfulness of your smile as the placement of gastric band has dropped half of the weight that you ever want to get rid of yourself

You are still losing a couple of inches off your body

(S.P after each of the above statements)

Take that shining light with your observation towards all the cells of your stomach

This stomach has lesser weight today than before

There are lesser layers of fat cells

There is a strong glittery shine that gives you hope and confidence

Let your cells relaxed a little bit more and breathe deeper as you imagine every inch of your skin

Your skin all around your body previously containing fat is healing

The healing is spreading from the centre of your body

At the centre, you have the gastric band and with that gastric band on your waistline you have power

(M.P after each of the above statements)

The gastric band's power is shining even brighter

The light is getting brighter and brighter that it fully covers your core and cells within your body

Feel the tightness of the gastric band, as the light gets brighter

The bright light calms down your senses and muscles with tightening of the gastric band around your tummy

The slightest tightening of the gastric band is gradually becoming thick

As you feel the small size gastric band is slowly pressing the skin of your stomach even closer to the back of your body

This gastric band is your favourite

The colour of the gastric band is your most desirable one

(S.P after each of the above statements)

Continue the picture of the gastric band in your imagination

The tightness of the gastric band is at an acceptable level

Allow yourself to relax

Your body is completely loose and the gastric band tightness is still allowing you to move flawlessly

This is another positive achievement of your appearance that the gastric band is tightened on your stomach and you are feeling happy

Take few steps ahead and embrace this change freely

With the flat stomach, the tightness of the gastric band is suitable for you to physically rest, turn and move, sit and walk

(L.PX2 after each of the above statements)

Your choice to accept a tighter gastric band is one of the best decisions for your health

The gastric band tightness increases your motivation to lose weight and burns even more fat residues

The tighter gastric band saves you from other methods

Your time is saved as you get to benefit from your tighter gastric band quickly and effortlessly

The gastric band is less complicated and full of ease

As you notice the tighter gastric band on your stomach your eating habits improve

Around your stomach, the gastric band enhances the feelings of fullness

(S.PX3 after each of the above statements)

There is a feeling of fullness and satiety following food consumption

The idea to tighten the gastric band is for you to lose weight

The tighter gastric band also helps in managing your excessive eating and binge eating episodes

The food you eat starts to digest absorbed and metabolized very easily

The gastric band is painless even in a tightening state

You consume your food without any distress whenever you feel hungry

You are wise to notice the signs of hunger and eat only when hungry

Your body is in shape and getting a lot more in shape to let you reach towards your ideal image

(S.P after each of the above statements)

Your body alarms you when full with the help of this gastric band you hold yourself back from excessive food consumption

You are accustomed to chewing every bite of your healthy food for at least 40 seconds before you ingest

You mindfully observe the food you eat

You take few bites and you swallow only nutritious food

The food meets your body requirements and you quickly notice that the tightness of the gastric band supports you in overcoming your food addictions

You are living a happy life with a flat stomach and the healthy fat is only present in your body

(S.P after each of the above statements)

Your body contains only healthy fat

There is a huge reduction in the food portions you eat

Your food plate only carries healthy food options

You do this in addition to your eating habits

As a result, you have observed that the tightness of your stomach is the most comfortable experience as if the leaves of the tree

Imagine you are spending a wonderful holiday near a treehouse

This treehouse is located within the large trees with fresh leaves

The unexplainable peace you experience near the trees complement your gastric band tightness

You are ready to enjoy these experiences

(L.P after each of the above statements)

Explore the treehouse and feel your stomach tightness

As you closely observe the leaves thickness and variety of shapes you smell the salty air coming from the nearby seaside

The beach is cool and the water is healing

Right after you listen to the waves of the sea

Imagine the touch of your stomach as a flat, slim and ideal figure

The wooden barks are rough like the rocky road but the visual sensations in your mind are enchanting

This place has a wide range of treats for you

(M.PX2 after each of the above statements)

Dig your feet into the warm soil, which is clear and clean

The earthlike taste is in your mouth that you are aware of

Collect all these relaxation-inducing experiences and appreciate the tightness of the gastric band around your belly

Once again with the sensory enrichment of the place you visualize

Bring yourself back to your environment from the core of your stomach

Following the counting from ten to one

You will be again present on your most comfortable piece of furniture

Ten

Nine

Eight

Seven

Six

Five

Four

Three

Two

One

Let the texture of your skin allows you to breathe in and breathe out deeply for three seconds

One

Two

Three

As you try to open your eyes feel the moments you cherish in the middle of the forests

You are back with more power and attention than before

You may sound more committed to your transformation whenever you speak

You must communicate and share the message of healing with others

Compassion is one of the best sources to get back what you want

Surround yourself with beautiful relationships and those who encourage you

Celebrate even the smallest milestones and assemble the shadows of blessings while let go of those that don't allure

(S.P after each of the above statements)

7. Do the mindful eating

Be comfortable in whatever position you are

Find a place where you can rest and lay down for a while

Focus on my voice as if there is no other voice coming into your ears

Feel the light and soft air around you

Close your eyes as if there is nothing to see

Wherever you are trying to keep your back and neck completely straight

Let your feet straight and loose

Let your palms straight and loose

Let your back straight

Focus on your hands, feet and backbone

Make sure they are all straight, loose and relaxed

(S.P after each of the above statements)

In whatever state you are in just observe

Avoid judgment but simply observe

When you complete observing you will be participating in your sensory experiencing and describing

So observe your weight on the floor or sofa on which you are resting

Observe your body from head to toe

Observe your sensations in your head

Observe your sensations in your forehead

Observe your sensations in your eyes

Observe your sensations around your nasal passage

Observe your sensations in your upper lips area

Observe your sensations in your chin and below your lips

Observe the sensations around your lips and ears

(S.P after each of the above statements)

In whatever state you are in just observe

Avoid judgment but simply observe

When you complete observing you will be participating in your sensory experiencing and describing

So observe your weight on the floor or sofa on which you are resting once again and now

Observe your neck area

Observe your sensations in your shoulders both right and left

Observe your sensations in your arms both right and left

Observe your sensations in your hands

Observe your sensations around your all ten fingers of both hands

Observe your sensations in your chest

Observe your sensations in your abdomen and hips

Observe the sensations around your legs, knees, ankles and feet till toes completely

(S.P after each of the above statements)

Completely allow yourself to reflect on your observations

Say a word about your scan of your head area

Say a word about the scan of your forehead

Say a word about the scan of your pair of eyes

Say a word about the scan of your nose

Say a word about the scan of your upper lips and lips

Say a word about the scan of your chin and the area under the chin

Say a word about the scan of your ears

Can you completely feel the sensations without any judgments like good or bad?

Be neutral in your description of sensations and say to yourself that you let go of judgments

Affirm, "I let go of judgments about myself and others or my food and body"

(S.P after each of the above statements)

Try again and completely allow yourself to reflect on your observations again

Say a word about your scan of your area around your neck

Say a word about the scan of your shoulders

Say a word about the scan of your arms and hands, fingers and stomach

Say a word about the scan of your chest and hips

Say a word about the scan of your legs and knees

Say a word about the scan of your knees and feet

Say a word about the scan of your toes

Can you completely feel the sensations without any judgments like good or bad?

Be neutral in your description of sensations and say to yourself that you let go of judgments

Affirm, "I let go of judgments about myself and others or my food and body"

(S.P after each of the above statements)

As you let go of your judgmental attitude and beliefs

You are welcome to go deeper and deeper in your reflection of the eating process

Feel as if there is a slide in front of you

The slide is colourful like a rainbow spread across your feet

The slide invites you to giggle

Imagine you are going down nicely and enjoying the slide that has led you into a house of flowers

(S.P after each of the above statements)

The house of flowers is an excellent place to master the skill of mindful eating

That is a habit to fully experience the food consumption process with the use of five senses completely

Pay attention with an open mind as if you have picked a free and fresh flower in your right hand

The flower is of your choice

The petals are very soft

The smell is exotic

The taste of the petal when you chew from your front teeth it is soothing

The blowing of the petals with cold air is an appealing view

(S.P after each of the above statements)

The flower is very beautiful you can observe the colours in it

You can describe the type of the flower, orchid maybe, sunflower, jasmine, lily and rose or any of your choice

The texture of the flower is shown differently in different parts to you like stem, centre, petals can be different

The smell may be stronger at certain parts of the flower

The taste may be better, sweet or tangy because the flower is edible and of good quality

(S.P after each of the above statements)

Eating mindfully means to eat with complete observation

Taking part in describing the sensory characteristics of the food you eat

This process includes eating appropriately based on the needs of the body

Just right in the amount, your body needs nutrients

Eat mindfully and you observe how you let go of any distractions and emotional burdens when you eat mindfully

This source of eating makes you healthier and wiser as you pick something to eat

Choose any food of your choice to practice the mindful eating

Make sure the food is healthy and something that you eat regularly or with more ease than the other options

(S.P after each of the above statements)

Overcoming challenges in healthy eating like addictive behaviours binge eating and excessive eating are all managed with the help of mindful eating

Mindful eating allows you to eat in small bites, slowly and chewing well to digest properly so that the absorption provides you maximum nutrition from the foods with highly nutritive values

(S.P after each of the above statements)

Let's get started with the mindful eating experience of food of your choice simply by flowing the experience you had with the flower of your choice in this house of flowers

Remember to fully experience your food consumption with the use of your five senses completely

Allow yourself to hold any seasonal and fresh fruit or vegetable in your right hand

The food is of your choice

The skin and peel of the food you hold in your right hand are very soft

The smell is exotic and the food is properly washed, clean and dry

The taste of the food when you take a bite from your front teeth is soothing

The bite taking from your teeth and chewing sound in between your jaw is exciting to hear

(S.P after each of the above statements)

The food you are holding in your hand is very appealing you can observe the colours in it and acknowledge that they are attractive

You can describe the form and shape of the food, long, short, round, small or big, large or any of your choice

The texture of the food that feels to you can be different like fluffy, mushy or pulpy, hard or coarse

The smell may be stronger, sweet or citric

The taste may be delicious, your taste buds enjoy it as the ripped and grown product of nature

(S.P after each of the above statements)

Take the best use of your imagination to observe the appearance of the food

Notice the colours, how many colours are there? Which ones? What are these colours? Are they darker? Light or pale or bright? Are there any lines on the food that you can observe? Any depths or any pressure?

As you have observed that now how do you describe, participate in a word that how is the food visually and what it means to you without any judgments

Take your time and describe for few seconds

1

2

3

4

5

Hope you are done

Now we can proceed further with the sensory experience of the food

(S.P after each of the above statements)

Take the best use of your imagination to observe the sound of the food when you eat

Take a small and gentle bite

Notice the bite as you get the tiny little portion of the food in your mouth

First, it touches your lips then you grab it tightly between the lips and pass it on to the teeth

That bite sound is unique and you take the bite in then chew and the whole jaw with tongue mixed in saliva churns down the food

As you have observed that now how do you describe, participate in a word that how is the food eating voices and what it means to you without any judgments

Take your time and describe for few seconds

1

2

3

4

5

Hope you are done

Now we can proceed further with the sensory experience of the food

(S.P after each of the above statements)

Take the best use of your imagination to observe the texture of the food when you touch and taste

How your skin on the hands feels the food when it comes in contact with it

Take a small and gentle bite again

Notice the feeling on your lips as you take a bite and the tiny little portion of the food in your mouth is mixed with a whole new process

First, it touches your lips it may give a soothing and pleasant sensation then you grab it tightly between the lips and pass it on to the teeth then this gives another texture of the food as you cut it down and try to tear to ingest

As you have observed that now how do you describe, participate in a word that how is the food eating textures that you felt and what it means to you without any judgments

Take your time and describe for few seconds

1

2

3

4

5

Hope you are done

Now we can proceed further with the sensory experience of the food

(S.P after each of the above statements)

Take the best use of your imagination one more time to observe the aroma and taste of the food when you touch and chew

How your nose finds the smell and feels the food when it comes in contact with it

Take a small and gentle bite again

Notice the original taste of the food and the juicy mouth secretions

As you have observed that now how do you describe, participate in a word that how is the food aroma and flavour that you experienced and what it means to you without any judgments

Take your time and describe for few seconds

1

2

3

4

5

Hope you are done

(S.P after each of the above statements)

As you have done very well in the practice of mindful eating

Affirm, "I am committed to eating mindfully whenever I eat and I accept that it is very helpful in managing my weight and keeping me slimmer, leaner and smarter"

Feel as if there is a staircase fully covered with flowers above your head like a crown to pass under it in front of you

The stairs are very bright and colourful like a rainbow spread across your feet

The slide invites you to giggle and takes you back into deep relaxation from the depths of your mindfully eating attitude

Imagine you are waking up from a dream with a new eating habit very nicely and cheerfully crossing below the shade of flowers from the house of the flowers

(S.P after each of the above statements)

Again, take your focus back on your body

Observe how you feel at your straight and loose feet

Observe how you feel at your straight and loose palms

Focus on your hands, feet and backbone

Make sure they are all straight, loose and relaxed again

Open your eyes as if there is relaxation everywhere

Feel comfortable in whatever position you are

Observe your entire place around you where you are resting at the moment

Focus on any voice that is coming into your ears

Feel the light and soft air around you

Enjoy healthy eating from today a lot more

(S.P after each of the above statements)

8. Improving body image, gaining more confidence and combating social anxieties

Close your eyes

Softly and gently

Let your head find a support

A soft and holding support that makes your neck straight and at ease

This is the time to receive something in your life for your health and wellness

To begin receiving join your hands and open them like a book

Nice, now hold the hands in this position facing your palms towards the ceiling

As you do this place the back of your hands on your stomach and imagine the gift is coming downward

Let's open the gift gradually

(M.PX3 after each of the above statements)

Own your gift and unwrap it

This is exciting and the procedure of unwrapping may be stimulating just like you experience any anxieties throughout the day

During your anxiety, the signs may be heart throbbing, sweaty hands, jerking and shaking, loss of energy and headache

Such experience might be an indicator of the fear of evaluation that emerges from the criticisms of other people about your body posture, physique and weight

A flabby stomach can be the reason or double chin

It is possible that some people are critical and some are just ignorant of the factors involved in this condition

There are our beliefs involved in the development of anxiety

The social anxiety that specifically appears in a social situation is related to the myths and assumptions that people don't like overweight bodies or they want to see only slim bodies

Such assumptions and myths are coped with with the help of helpful affirmations

These positive affirmations must be recalled daily

Affirm now "I have the ability and skills to achieve my goals for healthy eating and healthy weight without any fear of what people think of my body"

Now take a slow deep breath, inhale and exhale

Continue affirming with my voice and stay focused

I am free of any worry that people are watching me

I stay comfortable whatever the situation is

I do not worry about letting people watch me because I look beautiful and healthy

I stop worry whenever I step out of my room

I want to get freedom from my worries

I am beginning to overcome the anxiety and I learn to stay calm and peaceful

I relax whenever I get a chance to take a deep breath and I usually show compassion to myself by counting my deep breaths

A little progress in your condition each day is a blessing

Pay close attention to the state of your body and mind when it relaxes following the counting

The relaxation offers to you a healthy state of body and well mind

One at a time rule is the best way to get rid of workload and extra stress, pain or muscle tension

Do only one task at a time

Affirm "I am focused on my goal of mindful eating whenever I eat I quit all other tasks because the best taste is the feeling of being healthy"

As you learn to overcome the monsters of anxiety that were previously haunting you

The unwrapping of the gift is now becoming more pleasurable and slow with keen observation to take a look without any hurry or impulsivity

(M.PX3 after each of the above statements)

Listen carefully

Your body has allowed you to change the treatment you give to your body

Appreciate every inch of your body that has been transforming since the last few minutes

Your body deserved to be loved without any conditions and boundlessness

Affirm, "I love my body very much and I love my body with the treatment it deserves, I like every inch of my body and I am kind towards it all the time. Whenever I eat, I always notice how my body feels. This is an amazing feeling to be in love with my body. When I do something for my body I take care of its needs I feel better than before. My appearance is not what defines me, I am beyond the body, I am a soul and a kind heart I am compassionate and I am likeable, I survive as much life as possible and I am the whole new change that I work for every day. As a person, my body is unique and different from anyone else in this world. This is a gift a priceless gift to me"

Let another affirmation about body image influence your mind with great pleasure

Say with me and repeat "I honour my body as a sacred place where I can pray and charity, where I can show gratitude and love, where there is no such thing like negativity and associated words"

The body is a complete world for those who live in it but the real happiness is to live with it and to live for it

Imagine sending love and kindness to every cell of your body

To all the blood running in your bloodstreams

To all the fluids within

To all the organs functioning

To all the hormones and secretions that are own temple

Silently observe each of your body existing parts internally and externally to show thankfulness and loads of appreciation

You are now completely under the spell of your existence

Affirm "I open my heart to the beautiful and kind words that I use for myself, I say positive words for my body and I only appreciate how it functions, It is a blessing and I am grateful"

Notice how a spark of energy flows within you when you say nice and strongly positive words about yourself

This is the most precious gift that you offer to yourself and your body

The body image is the perception that a human being holds for self

The size and shape doesn't define self, only the perception of self matters

There is no one else who can do this for you

Only you know about yourself the best

Be the potential for your body-image

Be the world of your mind

Affirm "I have the best image of my body in my mind, I am carefree of the perceptions of anyone else, I know my body best and this is all that matters to me for a happy and satisfying life"

There is peace within me everywhere

I allow changes in my daily routine

I allow changes in my daily food

I allow changes in my daily meals

I allow changes in my activities

I allow changes in my thoughts, as they are more flexible now

I allow changes in my emotions as I can manage them wisely

I allow changes in my self-control as it is improved

I allow changes in my letting go attitude and I am more easily letting out the doubts, regrets and complains

I only allow my perception to define myself and my perception of my body is like a gift that I am receiving

I am opening the gift and this is my self that is sparkling, attractive and productive

This gift has to enlighten my mind and soul

My body is being praised and cared for with this gift

This is the outcome of this gift that I am holding that I love my body

(M.PX3 after each of the above statements)

Affirm, " I believe that I am getting more and more confident every day without any effort or distress"

I have the talent to express my thoughts politely towards myself

I am quite clever and clear in my mind about my confidence

I am aware of the wonderful functioning of my mind and body

I have vocabulary and fluency in my speech that has the power to influence my opinions

I am a good communicator to express my expression of admiration towards myself

I am a very confident person and an attractive soul

I love my personality traits as well like I deeply love my body

My love and likeness for my body and mind getting deeper and deeper and this is bringing me closer and closer to myself and my relationship with a healthy lifestyle is getting stronger and stronger

With this deep connection, the vibes of my motivation are spreading all around my body and my cells are all covered with the light, glow and joy of a healthy mind

This is the expression of deep and permanent confidence that is flowing within me

Anyone can witness the beauty of this confidence in my expression and communication, my physical movements, gestures and facial expressions

I feel so connected with my mind and the functioning of my body

As a spiritual being, I am open to the future gifts and blessings of the universe that are meant to reach my soul

This has been the awakening of my overall self and I exist to a wide array of positivity and beneficial range of world where my thoughts linger in search of even more confidence myself

Everything around me is spun like a silky threat of smiles

I am getting more and more relaxed and more and more confident as I realize that I am feeling very happy and grateful

Achieving confidence is a step of personal success as a vital sign to approach more opportunities

I am getting more and more confident as the days are passing

This is very special to me that this experience is multi-dimensional

I am honestly being in love with my beautiful and confident body like a vase that I bring to my room and place that at a higher place away from any hazards

That vase is the eye candy for everyone and the colours are very calming

This calming effect is my choice and I prefer everything in my life and for my health that is calming

Now let's get prepared for another part of this gift that you are holding in your hands, 1, 2, and 3

(M.PX3 after each of the above statements)

Remind yourself that "I let go of any addictions that didn't serve me ever because I am mentally strong and I know the importance of eating healthy and pure foods from the blessings of nature, I understand that the food I eat can cover only a small area in my stomach is the size of my fist and I manage to measure my meal based on my fist size.

On my plate, I always add a portion of fresh sliced or chopped coleslaw and greens, one portion of beans and only one portion from whole grains and lean meat"

As you find yourself vulnerable to falling into a loop of temptations and cravings for unhealthy food

There is always an option to enjoy a cheat meal, once in seven days or more

The food addiction or obsession with food is now resolved from within

I am pure and clean and feel sober like a new child

A new baby like steps I would like to take to hold the gift in my hand that I unwrapped

It is just as beautiful as the soft and tint of the skin a baby has

The gift is my health and wellness that is full of confidence, more and more confidence with an admiring body image

The gift supplied me with a life with clarity

The anxieties vanish and the addictive behaviours are gone away

The storms of the emotions and thunders of my stomach hunger pangs due to dieting or distress following excessive eating are now flowing like an obedient light that glows and glows spreading the hope all around my body and my skin reflects the glow from the light of hope

Affirm, "I feel as confidant as I am master my eating habits with self-control and wisdom"

(M.PX3 after each of the above statements)

Open your eyes

Softly and gently

Let your head turn right and then left

This is the time to say thank you openly and express gratitude for the gift of your health and wellness

To begin this expression join your hands together and close them like a book

Nice, now hold the hands in this position facing your palms towards each other and bow down your head a bit

As you do this gesture the outcome is the assurance that gifts stay with you forever

Let's take a deep breath showing gratitude to the universe

(M.PX3 after each of the above statements)

9. Removal of the gastric band

Get deeply relax

Imagine a shiny glass staircase is present in front of you

As you get more and more relaxed and comfortable at your place you will be able to move ahead smoothly

The footsteps that you will take might lead you to the lovely transformation of your body

You reach a newer version of yourself and your deep down desires may appear fulfilled

Desires about your body image and lesser fat, slimmer tummy and leaner you

You are going to witness your transformation today after few minutes

You might feel joy at your peak

(M.PX3 after each of the above statements)

Leave your body completely loose

Image your closeness to your created body as an outcome of the gastric band placement and tightening for the past few days

The wish of your soul is approaching completion

Starting a healthier life is an art that you have mastered

You have mastered this skill and now you are competent to eat healthy food and continue a slimmer life

Major changes in the past few days have dropped your weight to a remarkable level

With the help of the gastric band, your belly seems slimmer and smarter

Around your stomach, the skin glows and it feels tight with a complete youth

(S.PX4 after each of the above statements)

Take a deep nice breath again

Breathe in and out from the depths of your stomach

Let your body move according to your nasal passage contraction and relaxation

Your lungs take in the air and your mouth blows out the air in a pattern that you are watching regularly

Inhale as much as possible to the fullest capacity of your lungs

Let the lungs spread like a balloon and watch them rise for a few seconds, 1, 2, 3

Now continue focusing the system to exhale the air out for a few seconds, 1, 2, 3

(S.P after each of the above statements)

Very good, close your eyes tightly and imagine the staircase made of beautiful shining glass

The glass looks crystal clear, clean and transparent

You can see through the glass there are metal bars to support the stairs

The stairs are firm and glorious

The view is mind-blowing and for the next 10 seconds you will be moving downward using this staircase

As I count begin stepping on the first stair

1

Move to the next stair

2

Continue

3

Keep going

4

5

6

7

8

9

10

There is complete peace all around you

(S.P after each of the above statements)

Pay attention to where this staircase takes you

It is your favourite place

The same area where you took the initiative of this gastric band that has changed your lifestyle

Enjoy this feeling of accomplishment

Allow yourself to attract more and more blessings other than the desirable body weight and shape that the gastric band has given you

You have been offered to secure this achievement for the future

Throughout life, the slimmer and leaner belly stays with you

Without any doubt, you know this better than positivity transforms attitude towards food and our body

Your support to your body is the overall result of your gastric band

Your confidence, willpower, trust and determination has brought up this moment of success

Focus on the outcome of your body

There is a flat stomach and healthy-looking skin

(L.P after each of the above statements)

A healthy-looking feeling that you have is associated with your sensations of the gastric band effectiveness

It is easier for you now to keep moving with the same routine and lesser amount of food

You buy, choose, pick and prepare only nutritious and delicious food

Your experience with the gastric band is simply natural

This relationship has built because you have achieved the goals you settled at the beginning

Watch your radiance with the power of your mind

Your skin is smooth and supple

You are smaller in body size

You are in love with what you do

Visibly the vibes are your reality

(M.P after each of the above statements)

You feel your days are much more balanced similar to the food on the plate that you eat

Your amazing skill of choices and changes that you adopted for your health is appreciated

Your style of cooking and methods to mindfully get in touch with your food is a great progress

Your complete existence has shown a pretty smile

Listen to this your body is saying you thank you

Imagine the colour of your gastric band around your stomach

Place your hand on it and feel the band is of your favourite colour

The most suitable thickness and smallness of the gastric band compliments your tiny waistline

You can proudly say that you can keep this flat stomach daily in maintenance with your time and dedication towards a healthy lifestyle

The recommendations for your healthy eating are simple, quick and beneficial

You completely learn and educate yourself with the application process of the brave and bold task for eating healthy

(S.P after each of the above statements)

You are gratefully in love with the function of the gastric band that has now been completed successfully

You must proceed with the removal of the gastric band

For this purpose, you commit to your desired body weight and image that you would control your food amounts and calorie intake whenever you intend to consume a meal

You accept and agree with the free choice of eating healthy effortlessly and allow the removal of gastric band

Following this path to freedom and commitment simultaneously, every moment is a witness of your dedication to yourself

You share this genuine experience and feelings attached to the freedom from the burdens of your body

Imagine a vast limitless sight of the lake you know about

Next, the courage is going to increase without even the gastric band on your stomach

Your skin of the belly is smarter and lighter

(S.P after each of the above statements)

As the gastric band removes the skin becomes more sensitive to the air

Feel fresh as soon as the gastric band removes

The lightness of your belly might sound like a feather flying over the vast limitless lake

The responsible attitude of carrying the gastric band is shifting to the easiest commitment of maintaining healthy eating habits for a healthy body and mind

Your motivation strikes up as you make up your mind to create a big difference without the aid of the gastric band

Unlike the presence of a gastric band, you are capable to try creative ideas that lit up your intuition for improvement in overall health

The energy that you have gained is getting shinier and shinier

You have spread the light in the universe around you

Your shine vibrates and resonates with the skies

Your ability to forgive all those who ever criticize your body is getting flared up

The tendency to forgive yourself and others show that your tenderness and love is above all

You are talented enough to manifest your dreams into truth

The undeniable truth is that you eat as your body needs without the gastric band

(L.P after each of the above statements)

At a very slow pace

Show compassion to self and blow kisses to others in your imagination

You feel more and more relaxed

The deeply and deeply relaxed posture of yours like you to lose your muscles

As all the parts of your body relax the gastric band loses up as well

The gastric band is loosening for few seconds

1

2

3

4

5

6

7

Observe the motion of the gastric band

It's just slipping away from your skin

The soft procedure of the gastric band removal is painless and soundless

The only voice you hear for the next few seconds is of your peaceful deep breathing

1

2

3

Such a happy event has happened

(S.P after each of the above statements)

This happens due to what you like

Your preference has been strengthened for fresh ingredients like whole grains

The foods that all contain high nutritive value is your only preference to consume daily

Your stomach fills fast when you eat a smaller portion of food

You eat short meals and you nourish your body with lightweight naturally made snacks

(S.P after each of the above statements)

Imagine you love to chew corns for minutes

Boiled warm corns covered in herbs, chillies and lemon

This stimulates the smell of tangy flavours

The crunch and crisp is an essential part of your meal

The food equals the size of your fist and you feel full whenever you eat that food only in hunger

The foods you consume with minimum sugar intake, minimum fat content and minimum salt are the best for your mind and soul

Your body feels rested when you eat food at room temperature

You must facilitate your body with refreshing and metabolism-boosting beverages free of soda and artificial tasting

Our body reciprocates us

What we offer we get back

Give your body soul-enriching food

Drink mind and lemon

Blend yoghurt, fruits, raw veggies and honey

Drink milk and toss plain cheese on salads

Cut and slice the cucumbers, bell peppers, carrots and eggplants

Feel how you like the process of juices coming out

Smell how you get excited with the aroma

Know how you welcome the taste

See how you invite the variety

Listen to the knife on the cutting board when chopping the raw washed food helps your digestive system

As a healthy eater, the temperature of food to choose for storage and serving is all in your hands

Observe the strikes the crunchy and raw clean food make in your gums and jaw

This is so pure and it impresses your senses

(M.PX3 after each of the above statements)

Pay attention as if you look at the sky above a window in the dining room

The chair and table are of black wood

Your sight tries to catch the highest lengths of the sky where cotton balls like clouds are floating

It makes your cheeks blush and your lips going on a half-smile

Slightly spread the lips apart and murmur, "I love my body, I eat healthily, I eat clean and I eat raw, I eat in moderation"

Taking yourself back from the beautiful sightseeing's of your favourite place

Say goodbye to the generous gastric band

Look for the glass staircases that take you back from the depths of your transformation

Leaving behind the cold air, the noise of water and boats those move within

The glass staircase is not too far

(S.PX2 after each of the above statements)

Start walking and take small steps, these small steps also help you when you walk daily

The daily walk is one of the methods to maintain weight, to burn daily calories and to keep stomach slimmer

Be mindful as you take these steps on the road going to the stairs

As you observe walking steps, imagine the steady walking to open a new chapter of your life

A healthier life full of success and happiness is waiting for you to approach

Every morning or evening or anytime at least 30 minutes of walking can become an assurance of your healthy weight maintenance to meet your personal goals and to supply you with power

(M.P after each of the above statements)

Imagine the footsteps provide plenty of energy, courage, motivation and spark to stay on your health goals

Walk confidently, slowly; continue for few more minutes that direct your future

For young and older, for men and women for all ages and professionals, the walk is safe

You walk with complete comfort

As you walk, witness the comfort is flowing from your feet

From the base of your feet, the toes, heels and sole the comfort is on your ankles

The comfort is contagious, slow, deep and consistent

Notice the comfort pumps relaxation to the legs, above to the hips, above to your backbone and chest

It becomes more and more relaxing to walk and you can feel it in your chest and neck and shoulders and face

This is fine for you to walk for an hour and you become a regular walker within few days

(L.P after each of the above statements)

Now, look your staircase is right in your sight

The staircase is made of beautiful shining glass

The glass looks crystal clear, clean and transparent

You can see through the glass there are metal bars to support the stairs

The stairs are firm and glorious

The view is mind-blowing and for the next 10 seconds you will be moving upward using this staircase

As I count begin stepping on the tenth stair

10

Move to the next stair

9

Continue

8

Keep going

7

6

5

4

3

2

1

Open your eyes

There is complete peace all around you

(S.P after each of the above statements)

10.Continue healthy lifestyle

Find a comfortable place for you to rest

Straighten your back and limbs

Gather all the kind intentions for your body

Recall some of the smiling memories of yourself

Laugh out loud for your achievements so far

Open yourself for a new experience associated with your body

Your body weight is lighter

Your body image is ideal

Your body is now toned

The stomach fat has burned

You see your existence with excitement

Your excitement to continue receiving blessings for yourself remains the same

You are the witness of the shaping of your relationship with food into a healthier one

(M.PX2 after each of the above statements)

Relax your all body parts

Focus on your body parts one by one from head to toe

Progressively pay attention towards the relaxation of muscles and healthy cells functioning in each area of your body

Take a deep breath when you focus on your face muscles

Take a deep breath when you pay attention you're your relaxed neck and shoulders

Take a deep breath when you imagine that your chest muscles are relaxing

Take a deeper breath as you feel that your arms; hands, palms and fingers are relaxing

The energy is flowing from your shoulders to your fingernails

(L.P after each of the above statements)

Take a deep breath when you focus on your belly muscles

Take a deep breath when you pay attention you're your relaxed thighs and legs

Take a deep breath when you imagine that your hips and feet are relaxing

Take a deeper breath as you feel that your feet, heels, toes and sole are relaxing

The energy is flowing from your lower back to the end of your limbs

This progressive scan of your body muscles refreshes your ability to focus on your transformation

You are as much determined to maintain your body weight as much as you are relaxed and in love with your gastric band outcome

(S.P after each of the above statements)

Let your eyes closed slowly and naturally as you count from one to five

With each number, tighten your closed eyes

One for your eyes closed

Two for your eyes closing with tightness

Three for your eyes closed tighter and tighter

Four to feel that your eyes are now tightening and tightening even more

Five to leave your eyes closed as tight as possible

Coming down from your eyes to your chest

Breathing continues to relax your nerves

Pay attention to flow in and out of the air

Pay attention to the voice of your breathing

Pay attention to the texture of your skin above your lungs and stomach

(S.P after each of the above statements)

Feel the softness and smoothness of these body spots for your awareness

For three seconds just be grateful for whatever you have achieved so far

Aim to maintain and manage the achieved desirable state of body and mind

Imagine your lighter body is now capable of freely floating on a smooth and clear surface

Let your body fly in the air without any support

Imagine these sensations of touching air with your skin

Smell the air around your lighter body

Choose a colour to indicate the fluffy air surrounding your slimmer body

(S.PX3 after each of the above statements)

Allow the air to come near your ears and feel as if the clouds are spinning a web of mesh to support your body

Your hair is lighter in weight

Your head floats like a flower

Your cheeks are deeply soft and glowing

It appears that your face, your neck, upper body, lower body are all weightless

Like a cute balloon, you love this skydiving

Your muscles, cells and bones are weightless

Your stomach is lighter and smaller

At your complete resting state

You can make this position a routine for your self-discovery

Loosen your body completely once again and release all the things you usually hold

(L.PX4 after each of the above statements)

Take ten steps now from one to ten towards a new initiative of healthy eating as a lifestyle

Going down in the depths of your mind you are going to make healthy living a reality

Take step one and pay attention to the natural herbal fruits and vegetable farm downstairs

Take step two and you can smell the natural earthy smell of natural ingredients

Take step three and you can see fresh foods are ready for you to taste

Take further steps four, five and six so that you can grab the hanging fresh foods from the longer trees

At steps seven, eight and nine you can reach the herbal plants with exotic benefits

Put your feet on step ten and you can feel the raw texture of the soil

(S.P after each of the above statements)

Visit the whole farm and enjoy it

This healthy lifestyle is at the core of your mind where the belief takes rest

Leave yourself free in the middle of this farm and create beautiful memories

Associate yourself with the world's best available foods that are just grown from the earthly sources

This is the deepest place of your creative imagination

Where you learn to manifest a vast variety of raw foods and naturally made beverages

(S.P after each of the above statements)

Cherish each of the moments you stay here at this heavenly place

This farmland is limitless

The sounds you hear around you are the rustling of leaves

The soil particles are rich to enable nutritious foods to grow out

You experience freedom and you live like you have achieved all your goals related to body weight and healthy eating

Continue picking the fruits of your choice

The fruits that are fully packed with pulp and fibre

Pick the vegetables covered in soil to add to your daily meals

You have a routine to add the preparation of these naturally grown foods

(S.PX3 after each of the above statements)

You acknowledge the presence of these foods in your life

The air seems to dance and covering you all over

The smell of the fresh herbs continue

Your selection of being a part of this healthy life is aligned with your healthy life goals

You deserve appreciation for these accomplishments

You only add honey when you crave sweet

You make your sodium intake minimum per day about a pinch

You use herbal spices and lots of leaves over your salads

You eat clean and love the Mediterranean diet

Nuts and seeds daily enrich your smoothies and shakes

Continue nurturing yourself with these foods of great value

(S.PX2 after each of the above statements)

Make this choice of healthy food consumption a priority

Add daily walk for fast metabolism

Fast metabolism equals lesser fat storage on your belly

Prefer to chew whole grains, pulses and lentils, boiled beans and meat slices with egg

Stay with the use of cooking methods like grilling, boiling and roasting

Eat raw whereas possible

Eat till you feel full

Use hunger and fullness signals of your body in account to maintain the eating habits

Limit the intake of food when you feel full

Feel full with foods containing the higher nutritive value

(S.P after each of the above statements)

Enlist some snacks in the core of your mind and register them to use only when you crave in between meals

Limit processed foods and avoid any ready-made food consumption

Enjoy the food only in their true sense

Imagine yourself handling a handful of natural food items for each meal

The portion contains green leafy vegetables, fibre rich foods and some other varieties of your preference

Your dairy portion is necessary

Include a cup of yoghurt or milk or other dairy made recipes in each of your daily meals

Your day become purely delicious

For breakfast sometimes boil protein sources and sometimes mix a bowl of oats with warm milk

(M.P after each of the above statements)

Now try the addition of some crisp in your foods

The crunch of the veggies in rainbow colours

Purple, green, orange, yellow and blue

Make sure you add all in a week

Toss some corn and olives with while meat and lean cuts they are also very healthy

The choice is yours

Only options are discussed

Serve yourself the food at a room temperature

You stay focused

Your focus is health

The snacks are your favourites

You resist all artificial flavours and colours

You resist junks

Lower down the fats, salt and sugar

Energy bars are excellent to chew

Chew till you completely enjoy the textures, juices and smell mindfully

(L.P after each of the above statements)

Affirm " I am a healthy eater daily"

Affirm, " I am getting slimmer and slimmer, leaner and leaner"

Affirm, "I can manage my eating and I control the unnecessary temptations"

You know very well that healthy foods are the secret of your weight management

Your choice of food is your fuel

For instant energy, you always eat something light and loaded with nutrients

You drink plain water most of the time

Your daily intake of water is 10 glasses

Continue imagining the attainment of all those foods that are in your access and good for your mental and physical health

(S.P after each of the above statements)

As a healthy eater, you are passionate about the preparation of food at home

The recipes are in your access

You keep the dishes simple and ingredients less

You make the food with your own hands so that you make sure that you stick to the healthy goals regularly

This is an easy task to know what foods are good for health and what we can eat daily

Feel the freshness and glow on your face and skin all over your body

You are getting lighter and lighter as you eat

Affirm, "I am getting healthier and healthier as I follow healthy dietary habits"

As much as you are satisfied with the healthy food choices for yourself you stay healthy

You are capable of keeping your weight in moderation

Eat-in moderation and track your weight once a month

Write some notes whenever you feel there are some challenges

The answers to cope with the challenges comes from the core of your mind

Your healthy eating practice is good for your smart, thin, pretty and flat belly

Your tummy only invites food that is according to your needs

You have the strength to take healthy steps for yourself

You feel beautiful as an outcome

(S.P after each of the above statements)

Water has become your best drink

At this farm, you explore the healthy lifestyle

The lifestyle that continues to be your preference

You enjoy whole foods and colourful natural' gifts

Clean the food that you buy to eat raw

Wash the foods properly and your hands as well

The foods with high water content are very refreshing

They have a cooling effect like the open farmland

The direct sun gives hope and happiness

The fresh air let you breathe to your fullest

The cells of your body functions multiply and replace all the time

Healthy food cleanses you and removes all the toxins

Healthy food flushes out your unrequired impurities

(S.P after each of the above statements)

The place where you are present at the moment

Imagine it with complete focus

Watch out all the sides of the land

Wherever you see you see the bliss

The sky has a blue hue above you

Clouds are floating peacefully there is calmness all around

The quietness has the appearance of the foods only

Be mindful of what you eat daily

Continue to follow the routine of healthy food choices

Pick those foods always that are natural and nutritious

Your food consumption do meet your body needs without adding an excessive burden

(S.P after each of the above statements)

This is your future your healthy routine has become your destiny

As you realize you have lived these moments completely

Begin moving towards the soil-filled staircase

The staircase is ready for you to move back upwards

As you listen to the counting ten to one flow your mind in a smooth manner

Take the first step on the tenth stair

Now one step more and you are on nine

Eight

Seven

Continue climbing

Six

Five

Four

Three

Two

One

A new morning awaits you

Get yourself out of the depths of your mind and get settled to open your eyes very very slowly

(S.P after each of the above statements)

Keep it up you do a marvellous discovery to monitor your mind

Be in harmony with your healthy goals

This journey has remained successful all the time

Wish you satisfaction ahead

Every day and every second

You have made this choice

Your life is healthy

Eating is healthy

Shopping is healthy!

(S.P after each of the above statements)

11.Work on taking the food and eating in your control

Its time to place your hands and arms in the most comfortable position and place as you can

Its time to relax and listen to the only voice that is directly in contact with you to allow you to relax

Let this voice guides you to become more and more deeply and deeply relaxed

Let me show you that you hear this voice to direct you to a more self-control

Take your time and close your eyes whenever you feel best

In the next few moments, you would be laying down with the most peaceful and calm body

(L.P after each of the above statements)

So, in short, you are helping yourself with following this voice

As you continue listening silently and without any other sound your breathing comes to your awareness

Breathing is a beautiful phenomenon and it flows naturally in a continuous rhythm

As you might have an idea that breathing is not in our awareness because we stay busy and keep our minds involved in many other things but today let yourself be aware of your breathing

Breathe fully, freely, deeply as much as you can

For the next few seconds practice this without any judgment

Let your nasal sounds speak

(L.P after each of the above statements)

Prepare yourself for alternate nostril breathing

This is one of the most soothing ways to treat you with kindness

The kindest act that we ever do is to let go of all the pain and stress so that we can sleep and rest restfully

Take your right hand to your nose and with the help of the index finger press the right nostril to inhale from the left nostril

Now, leave and shift your finger to press the left nostril and exhale from the right nostril

I believe you are a quick and smart learner, let's repeat once again

Take your right hand to your nose and with the help of the index finger press the right nostril to inhale from the left nostril

Now, leave shift your finger to press the left nostril and exhale from the right nostril

Great, time to take your left hand to your nose and with the help of the index finger press the left nostril to inhale from the right nostril

Now, leave and shift your finger to press the right nostril and exhale from the left nostril

I believe you are a quick and smart learner, let's repeat once again

Great, time to take your left hand to your nose and with the help of the index finger press the left nostril to inhale from the right nostril

Now, leave and shift your finger to press the right nostril and exhale from the left nostril

(S.P after each of the above statements)

By doing this practice, you can switch your body and mind to a relaxed state whenever and wherever you can

Relaxation is a priority and key to maintaining a behaviour

There may be 100's of voices that you hear daily but the only voice that matters is the voice of your soul

The inner voice is the most reliable, the trustworthy, and the most melodious

(M.P after each of the above statements)

In the depths of your soul, there is a place where self-control is activated

Get down in the depths of your soul

Imagine there is a staircase leading you to the unknown secrets of your self-control activation

With my voice imagine the movement of your feet going down straight to the depth of your soul from

As I count from 1-10, imagine going downstairs keeping your attention in the middle of your chest where your heart is beating

1, 2, 3, 4, 5, 6, 7, 8, 9, 10 (S.P between each)

Now you are at the depth of your soul and a cool blue, peaceful light ball is in front of you

Continue to breathe deeply; the light ball is your self-control, ready to take in your hands

(M.P after each of the above statements)

As you relax, imagine a picture in your mind where you idealize your personality as a person who is an example of the best self-control

Self-control is strength, there is strength in the control that you take on yourself, on your obsessions about excessive eating, on your emotions letting you eat without any need and self-control is also your mood to monitor your food intake and to remind yourself that it is important to abide by the commitment of healthy eating, slimmer stomach and leaner fat-free body for the rest of your life

(L.PX2 after each of the above statements)

Focus on purpose is the foremost condition of self-control

Most of the impulsive decisions and actions we take under the influence of our irrational thoughts and negative emotions are not related to our food intake and also have no relation to the appetite

Let the purpose be your sole guide to empower you to seek, ask and practice self-control without any force and external pressures

Shed out all those moments from your memory when someone else actions and comments made you lose your self-control

You are intelligent and you direct your significant journey of maintaining a healthier weight, slimmer body shape and glowing skin with the help of self-control while you consume food and drink water

(M.P after each of the above statements)

Beating temptations is another milestone for self-control

One way to beat temptations is consistency with discipline

Eating and drinking on a fixed schedule can help

It can be flexible based on your feasibility and routine

Do what matches your life and develop a higher character of self-control

Step up in your power of seeking self-control and practising it whenever you mindlessly linger your eyes on unhealthy food

Be mindful of the triggers and choose an action to cope with it

(L.P after each of the above statements)

Overcome the unpredictable actions by planning eating time and foods with appropriate quantity in advance

This is the quality that you add to your eating habits

There are many faces of self-control that you learn here

The moment you decide to take hold your conscience helps you

There is no need to talk to anyone, do a private speech meditation of few seconds for the support

Just try it right now, pick a word for your ease to verbalize when you are in the need of self-control

It may be bind, it may be fixed or comes back

After you choose, repeat your selected word five times

Now count your fingers of the right hand

Now count your fingers on the left hand

Wow! You just delayed your gratification for the whole 15 seconds

This is what you need whenever you need self-control

A break and pause of 15 seconds is shown to release the momentary temptation

Just look away from the temptation for 15 seconds

Stay as far away as you can where there is no aroma of the temptation

This is the formula to your willpower too

(M.P after each of the above statements)

Another self-control tactic is improving stamina with the help of daily movements

The movements need to be easy

Quick and short

You can move your body as you want

Try Zumba, join a dance class, go on a walk with a friend or shake your body with the help of a song alone

(M.P after each of the above statements)

Whenever you move your body and stretch a bit you realize it is supplying even more brightness and colour to your blue self-control ball with power, patience and delayed action

Affirm with your body movement "I move my body and experience self-control"

(M.P after each of the above statements)

Other pleasurable activities might help you as well

Keep an activity diary with you wherever you go

Include a list of 10 exciting mind-diverting activities that give you self-control to maintain your focus on self-control over food

Something that stops your cravings

Read a joke, share a quote, write something interesting, take a photo and delete it, these tasks are at no cost but saves you 100's calories

Always take a big water bottle in your bag and drink 10 cups per day

Water manages weight and cravings before appetite signals as well

Only eat when the empty stomach and enjoy life lightly

(M.P after each of the above statements)

Look for what's in your plate that contains protein and much of it to cover the unnecessary fats and sugar that leads to excessive eating

Skip the alcoholic beverages and cut down the packaged juices

With these tips, you would see a visible difference in your ability to manage your trend towards eating unhealthy foods to a great extent

There is sufficient research evidence to convince someone

When you distance yourself from food within meal gaps and outside fixed schedule for meals you can drop down the harm from 50-60%

(M.P after each of the above statements)

Maintain energy levels

Let me explain another secret to managing self-control when food is present around you and there is no appetite for that food exist in your body

Always chew some energy bars, take a zip-lock bag with fruit, dates or nuts to avoid extreme hunger pangs for a longer time

As you stay away from food somewhat fill your stomach so that you usually don't get back to food without boundaries when available

The body needs food on time to prevent the excessive storage of food following longer times of empty stomach

Maintain a reciprocal relationship with your body and mind

Let them take care of you in exchange for providing them with care

(M.P after each of the above statements)

Build associations between the work and relaxation by connecting them with stress-busting activities

Stress anchors excessive eating and stress management means no cravings and less eating

It is always a great idea to connect your stress with a healthy food bite

Take an example of spinach, equals to the size of your smallest finger, chew it for at least 60 seconds

Observe and describe the taste, smell, colour and texture

Listen to the jaws churning up and juices of your saliva getting mixed with it

All the stress vanishes away and for few seconds you find a soothing trick for your nerves

(M.P after each of the above statements)

Review upon the self-control methods you have learned today

The understanding of these methods gives you more and more deep insight about using them

Be flexible and find several different ways to soothe you daily so that the mind stays relaxed as the relaxed mind keeps control of the actions and act logically for a health-oriented lifestyle

Take proper sleep and make a proper meal plan

Review your plan weekly and make adjustments whereas necessary to cope up with the circumstantial changes and unavoidable life challenges

(M.P after each of the above statements)

Observe deeply the blue light ball that is present in your hands

You are taking it back with you out of your soul

The activation of the blue light ball has been done as you progressively learn the tactics to practice self-control

The ball is very powerful and you can always take it in your hands with closed eyes whenever you lose control and search for something to get back to self-control

(M.P after each of the above statements)

The same staircase is going upward in the form of 10 stairs (S.P)

You may climb up towards the external world, one at a time, slowly and with peace 1, 2, 3, 4, 5, 6, 7, 8, 9, and 10 (S.P between each number)

Deep breathe as you are out of that staircase with the blue light ball of self-control in your hands that you have gained well now

You have reached the place from where we moved ahead to the glorious success of achieving your health-related goals

Open your eyes to the physical objects that are present around you as you have formed required habits and self-control is now your strength

(M.P after each of the above statements)

Conclusion

Hypnosis is a science and so does the weight loss and associated biochemical or psychosocial processes. The benefits of using hypnosis for weight loss are numerous. The first and foremost effect of using hypnosis is deep relaxation. Then there comes the formation of the habit for healthy eating, picking nutritious food without compromising delicious tastes and flavours. For some people, all these changes come slowly than others. The rate of change may be related to the willingness and motivation that the person shows who follow this method of healing eating problems. Hypnosis works for all different when it comes to weight loss.

Weight loss isn't any magic trick; there is no magic wand to spread a chant for a healthy eating lifestyle. There is sufficient evidence to plan diets and follow foods to avoid list for fat burn and weight management but there is no guarantee that a person is motivated and willing enough to comply with the given instructions on a piece of paper unless someone deliberately believes that the diet would help them. Weight loss is not only a matter of self-control but also a way to feel happiness and satisfaction. An ideal weight elicits the self-image in a person's mind to support further performance in one's occupational and personal life. We continue eating the ideal way possibly and automatically. Weight loss is not the only benefit with the help of gastric band hypnosis. Other benefits are overcoming emotional eating, dealing with malnutrition, getting rid of the foods that are harmful to human beings, improving self-image and nutritious eating habits development. There are many more psychological and social benefits that individuals may experience with time. The outcomes frequency and benefits differ from individual to individual because everyone is unique. Gastric band hypnosis is a useful tool that is even more powerful than the already observed. This is usually the beginning of lifetime learning with a purposeful plan with documented literature.

Weight loss is a proven outcome of hypnosis and related techniques that we associate and use with this method. Most commonly the notable results are specific to some people's contexts. Studies have shown that those who are more responsive to the hypnosis effect are compassionate, open to new experiences and selfless lovers. Personality traits play a role in the ease of the change process. On the other hand, the more susceptible people to hypnosis are below 18 or above 40. Within gender differences, females are more drawn to hypnosis than males.

On the other hand, people are more likely to be hypnotized if the hypnotist voice and way of communication is well-practised, according to the client needs and he or she guides appropriately. Change and weight loss are the processes. That is why; we use an integrative approach to maximize the outcome and optimal human pleasure without compromising the food or abiding by any tiring routine. Another component added to the series of this book is maintaining weight after required loss and fat burning sessions to take the most advantage of hypnosis for this purpose. Good Luck!

Reference Resource Links

1. https://www.jqph.org/index.php/JQPH/article/view/150
2. https://www.sciencedirect.com/science/article/abs/pii/S1130862119301159
3. https://link.springer.com/chapter/10.1007/978-1-4939-9098-6_17
4. http://www.ijnhs.net/index.php/ijnhs/article/view/317
5. https://www.sciencedirect.com/science/article/abs/pii/S0169260715304399
6. https://search.proquest.com/openview/f3bba7b5d087324407284cee65ee84fe/1?pq-origsite=gscholar&cbl=3912278
7. https://www.tandfonline.com/doi/abs/10.1080/08964289.2020.1842316
8. https://www.tandfonline.com/doi/abs/10.1080/00207144.2017.1314740
9. https://onlinelibrary.wiley.com/doi/abs/10.1002/acp.3730
10. https://www.intechopen.com/books/hypnotherapy-and-hypnosis/hypnosis-and-hypnotherapy-emerging-of-science-based-hypnosis
11. https://www.tandfonline.com/doi/abs/10.1080/00029157.2017.1316233
12. https://www.tandfonline.com/doi/abs/10.1080/00029157.2018.1489777
13. https://www.liebertpub.com/doi/abs/10.1089/acm.2020.0104
14. https://www.tandfonline.com/doi/abs/10.1080/00029157.2016.1261678
15. https://www.emerald.com/insight/content/doi/10.1108/JOE-07-2019-0029/full/html
16. https://onlinelibrary.wiley.com/doi/abs/10.1111/obr.13003
17. https://www.tandfonline.com/doi/abs/10.1080/00207144.2019.1613863
18. https://iris.unito.it/handle/2318/1633448#.YHVRp2hRXUo
19. https://ijbmc.org/index.php/ijbmc/article/view/174
20. https://search.proquest.com/openview/d75a70ca3c69b5537a40ffe7dd856030/1?pq-origsite=gscholar&cbl=1896353
21. https://onlinelibrary.wiley.com/doi/abs/10.1002/9781119057840.ch159
22. https://psycnet.apa.org/record/2018-03961-001
23. https://onlinelibrary.wiley.com/doi/abs/10.1002/oby.22262
24. https://www.sciencedirect.com/science/article/abs/pii/S1879729620301496

CPSIA information can be obtained
at www.ICGtesting.com
Printed in the USA
LVHW061945180521
687789LV00003B/632

9 781801 348287